What people are say

Furnace of this World; or, 36 Observations about Goodness

Against the assumption that to look for and find goodness in today's world is either dangerous, or naive, or both, comes Ed Simon's *Furnace of this World*. This exuberant and erudite collection insists on the paradoxical power of good to exist where we least expect it. Embracing both Broadway and Bonhoeffer, AA and Augustine in its expansive geography of goodness, Simon's work is profound, often heartbreaking, yet surprisingly cheering.

Brook Willensky-Lanford, author of *Paradise Lust: Searching for the Garden of Eden*

Reading Ed Simon's *Furnace of this World.* is like pausing for an hour [...] to listen to a wise stranger who is equal parts poet, prophet, and philosopher. You will be quiet, you will be rapt – and you will never be the same.

J.C. Hallman, author of *B & Me: A True Story of Literary Arousal*

Between the struggle for religious certitude and stick-in-the-mud atheism is Ed Simon's honest and authentic exploration of the language of morality. Simon presents narratives of faith and doubt from across literature to instruct the reader that literalism in any form will never bring us as close to a well-lived life as the simple and quiet search for the good.

Peter Bebergal, author of *Strange Frequencies*

Ed Simon's writing is perfectly suited to his theme, and reflects his preoccupations as a deep, wide-ranging and generous reader and thinker who applies his skills to address the fundamental question of human goodness.

Lydia Kiesling, editor at *The Millions* and author of *The Golden State*

Furnace of this World; or, 36 Observations about Goodness

Furnace of this World; or, 36 Observations about Goodness

Ed Simon

Winchester, UK
Washington, USA

JOHN HUNT PUBLISHING

First published by Zero Books, 2019
Zero Books is an imprint of John Hunt Publishing Ltd., No. 3 East St., Alresford,
Hampshire SO24 9EE, UK
office@jhpbooks.com
www.johnhuntpublishing.com
www.zero-books.net

For distributor details and how to order please visit the 'Ordering' section on our website.

Text copyright: Ed Simon 2018

ISBN: 978 1 78904 125 5
978 1 78904 126 2 (ebook)
Library of Congress Control Number: 2018943952

A CIP catalogue record for this book is available from the British Library.

Design: Stuart Davies

UK: Printed and bound by CPI Group (UK) Ltd, Croydon, CR0 4YY
US: Printed and bound by Thomson-Shore, 7300 West Joy Road, Dexter, MI 48130

We operate a distinctive and ethical publishing philosophy in
all areas of our business, from our global network of authors to
production and worldwide distribution.

Also by the Author

America and Other Fictions, Zero Books, 2018
ISBN 978-1-78535-845-6
The Anthology of Babel, Punctum Books, 2018

Dedicated to Matt Simon

Imaginary evil is romantic and varied; real evil is gloomy, monotonous, barren, boring. Imaginary good is boring; real good is always marvelous, intoxicating.
Simone Weil, Gravity and Grace

You are not obligated to finish the work, but neither are you free to desist from it.
Pirke Avot (2:21)

To hear the faint sound of oars in the silence as a rowboat/comes slowly out and then goes back is truly worth/all the years of sorrow that are to come.
Jack Gilbert, A Brief for the Defense

Introduction: Against Theology

I hold no truck with systems. The greatest prophet ever produced on Albion's shores in that green & pleasant land was the Romantic poet William Blake, and he said something quite similar: "I must create a system, or be enslav'd by another man's." The utility in the perennial creation of said systems is that it reminds us that they're always inventions; ingenious and often beautiful constructions of metaphors which endlessly defer, and that only sometimes correspond to reality. To point out that systems – religion, metaphysics, theology, what have you – are constructions is not to necessarily denigrate them, but to always remember that they're ever shifting, ever mercurial, and often relative in their definitions. Free play in systems, and some wisdom too, but it's easy to confuse them for the thing itself, which in their infinite understanding the ancient prophets understood to be idolatry.

As such, I make no claims that *Furnace of this World* is complete, rigorous, rational, logical, consistent, or universal; nor should the reader be confused by the presence of stated "axioms" throughout the course of the narrative. The subtitle contains the word "observations" for a reason, with all of the connotations of contingency and relativism which that word implies, because I do not claim to be constructing any sort of consistent ethical system, rather these are a few philosophical musings which I hope might do someone else some good. In writing my observations about goodness I neither claim the mantle of being an expert on ethics or morality, nor do I claim myself to even be a particularly good person. Rather I present this work as the moral equivalent of a *Wunderkammer* – a "Wonder Cabinet" – that is a collection of strange occurrences, theories, philosophies, narratives, and fictions which in some way I hope alludes to a perspective on the world, and succor attending to the question of how an individual is supposed to conduct themselves with the finite amount of time we have (and please note that while most of the book does recount actual personages, the 23rd fragment details a character of my own invention).

To claim that ours is a particularly cruel era would evidence either a lack of scholarly rigor or naivety at best, wanton ignorance at worst. One need only familiarize oneself with the horrors of the Middle Passage, the early modern wars of religion, the colonial genocides of that same time period, or the details of the Holocaust to understand that there never was any Eden, and that the Fall has always been now. Fashionable among traditionalists to pretend that ours is a uniquely awful age, though one should rather be skeptical of those that pine for some idealized past that never was. Mistrust in myth of a Golden Age is sober and respectable, it keeps one honest and aware that those who promote legends of an idyllic past often have in mind a terrible future. But in rejecting the vagaries of wistful conservatism which conveniently ignores the atrocities, one should equally chart a course away from the optimistic positivists like psychologist Steven Pinker who sunnily argues that things have been only getting better since the advent of morality, and who in 2011's *The Better Angels of our Nature* could claim that "The world has far too much morality" (as if we had much to spare).

Those of that particular ilk, the cyber utopians, techno-advocates, transhumanists, and the rest of the assembled positivists valorize the present at the expense of the past, but often their desire for the future is just as malignant as that of the reactionary who places their Kingdom of Heaven in the past. For men (and it normally takes a man to pretend that everything in the present is perfect) ours is the veritable Golden Age, where the steady progress of science and capitalism will join hands and march forward to ever more perfect futures. Pinker makes the argument that the world is less violent in the present than at any point in our history, a dubious assertion which relies on ignoring the latent violence inherent in the possibility that all of us could be incinerated in a nuclear conflagration at any instance – a violence which I should add that no medieval woman or man suffered under, no matter how uncouth their table manners may have been.

The reactionary may valorize the past, and the positivist the present, but it takes the imagination of the radical to rather truly valorize the future, which is what I pray that I'm able to do. Problem is, I'm never entirely certain that a better future is possible, only that the past and the present always come up short when compared to the greatest striving of our nature. Maybe it's radicals of a better caliber than me who can pine for the "immanentizing of the eschaton," as historian Eric Vogelin may have put it, but I've always suspected that though Utopia may exist, it's sadly always in a direction to which we can't point. In *Candide* Voltaire famously dismissed all manner of optimistic attempts to reform the word with the injunction that it is best to "tend his own garden." Despite the French atheist's reputation for radicalism, such an assertion has often been the declaration of the conservative. From Edmund Burke onward, the conservative (distinct from the rightist) has had suspicion of change at the center of their perspective, perhaps more an emotional state than an ideology, but a perspective all the same.

In my writings I've often counter-intuitively displayed my own doubts about ever being able to reach the shores of Utopia, much less that I'll ever be a permanent citizen of that imagined land. In *America and Other Fictions*, I wrote that "liberals assume that everyone is good and rational but just hasn't read the right *Mother Jones* article or heard the right NPR broadcast yet," and while I'm loathe to commit the vulgar, fallacious conflation of the centrist liberal with the leftist, I do believe that an undue faith in reason can be the failing of both. That might sound conservative, as if I'm putting my lot in with those who think the Kingdom of

Heaven can never be established on this Earth, but where I differ is that I've no doubt that Utopia is a real place – I just doubt that we can ever get to it. Semantics? Perhaps, but Utopia, like all good things, be it God or goodness, can be real and can affect us and can define our lives and our behaviors, without us ever having the ability to categorize, map, or outline their reality. Or maybe they don't even have to be real to be good. God after all might just be the most influential fictional character who ever existed.

I rather proposed the emergence of a "left Augustinianism," that is a method of radical politics and critique which is indebted to Augustine's sense of original sin, that is which admits to a certain (metaphorical) fallenness whose acknowledgment keeps us honest. *Furnace of this World* is not meant as an analytical explication of left Augustinianism per se, though it's born out of the same sense of limitation. If anything, with its digressive, fragmented, incomplete nature, *Furnace of this World* is most in keeping with the ideas I explored as concerning left Augustinism, in that the very form of this short book embodies what I hope is the humble, incomplete, uncertain approach to something as grand as "goodness." As with the idea behind left Augustinianism, with its doubts about ever reaching Utopia but the steadfast insistence that we must always try. The "axioms" I put forward in *Furnace of this World* are thus to be read precisely as being the "observations" the subtitle indicates, as flexible, contingent, hypothetical conjectures. Mine is, thank God, not some sort of ethical system, there is no categorical imperative here nor any utilitarian calculus in the manner of Jeremy Bentham. Remember, I hold no truck with systems.

That's not to say that I don't take my claims seriously here – I very much do. But the open-ended, theoretical nature of the endeavor is precisely the point, it's in keeping with a different claim I also made in *America and Other Fictions* that "the fact that Utopia itself can never be reached is not to advocate for an abandonment of utopianism." In that sense *Furnace of this World* and my writings about left Augustinianism and utopianism are part of the same theoretical project, the acknowledgment of the usefulness of certain models when we are suspicious of certainty (albeit those earlier projects traded in politics and this in ethics – as if those two are easily separated). At the core of such a suspicion of certainty is the very generic form of the piece itself, for in making my "observations" as if in a notebook, as if I were finding an interesting shell or an ancient relic pressing into the service of my moral *Wunderkammer*, I'm trying to exhibit the very anti-systematic nature which marks that other work.

What I try to convey through *Furnace of this World* is what could be called an "apophatic ethics," indeed one could claim that left Augustinianism is an "apophatic politics" or my literary criticism in other articles evidences an "apophatic aesthetics." In this book you'll encounter several Greek phrases, what's one more theology term at the outset? The term "apophatic" refers to a particular approach towards the language which concerns God, one that is popular in the Eastern Rite traditions, but is also evident in the Latin West to a lesser extent. Apophasis refers to one approach to understanding divinity and the transcendent, and it contrasts with its opposite, "kataphasis," which sees no issue with making clear declarations about the nature of God, and which defines the mainstream of what most people think of as "religion."

Apophatic approaches to God broadly believe that it is impossible to make any positive declarations about God; so that the phrase "God is good" is nonsensical to the advocate for apophatic theology, more accurate to simply say "God is not not good." For those mystical minded theologians who doubt the veracity of corresponding truth claims a concept such as God is too ineffable to be fully circumscribed in principles, for to even say that "God exists" is to make an idol out of words – for the apophatic such a seemingly unobjectionable claim for most of the faithful is literally non-sensical. As the twentieth-century theologian Paul Tillich wrote, "God does not exist. He is being itself beyond essence and existence. Therefore to argue that God exists is to deny him."

In the Catholic and Protestant West this method is sometimes known as the *via Negativa,* which hold that language regarding claims about God must always be phrased with an awareness as to the limitations of our definitions of God. In *America and Other Fictions,* I advocated for a "type of *via Negativa* approach to utopianism, a means of holding in our mind's eye the possibility of utopia and charting an ever and ever closer course towards her shore, even if the strand must always in some sense be inaccessible," and I argue that a similar apophatic pose can be applied not just to politics, but ethics and aesthetics as well. That is to say, again, that I firmly hold to the enduring power of certain metaphors while taking pains to understand that, to quote Ludwig Wittgenstein, "Whereof one cannot speak, thereof one must remain silent."

What results is a proudly inexact, paradoxical, perhaps confused and confusing set of observations, ones where I very dearly hold to the necessity of goodness without being able to simply define what it is. This, it seems to me, is far from being mere diversionary nonsense, and is rather estimably reasonable. Throughout the entirety of my writing I am a firm advocate for the use of theological language as a mode of political critique, both in a practical and an analytical sense. But the risk of any such advocacy – the risk of resurrecting words like "good" and "evil" – is that much of the later has been justified by recourse to the former. There is a danger of becoming Manichean in our reasoning, and to bracket out anything as indicative of "goodness" poses the possibility of ironically doing the exact opposite. As such, I believe in that *via Negativa* method in approaching goodness, an apophatic ethics, where I heartily affirm the existence of something called "goodness" even if I'm not always exactly sure what it is.

Such humility doesn't preclude me from generating the previously mentioned "axioms" about goodness. None of these are to be read as immutable laws of any sort, and God forbid reading them as self-help. I've no desire or aptitude to be a guru in that way, and loath is the academic charlatan who thinks that a smattering of Jungian psychobabble and some sociobiology can provide any sort of code to life. No, I rather prefer my admitted charlatanry to be of a more modest nature, and so take these axioms as more the bullshit session observations of someone who firmly hopes, prays, and sometimes believes that goodness is an actual thing, and that we'll have to find it if we're to have any hope of saving ourselves.

Best to leave their explication for the book itself, as this volume basically serves as an exegesis on them, but for the impatient among you they include the claim that "Goodness is never circumscribed by law, or literalism, or mere metaphysical speculation, it is only defined by compassion," that there is a "non-totalizing power of goodness" where goodness is good not in spite of its modesty, but because of it, and that sometimes goodness is "expressed with denying official teaching...sometimes goodness is manifested by denying God's commandments," among other implicit and explicit ventures. I try to explain such assertions with recourse to radical Death-of-God theology, apophatic rhetoric, Lurianic kabbalah, theories of universal salvation, the Twelve Steps of AA, literary examples from Flannery O'Connor to Joyce Carol Oates, the poetry of Jack Gilbert (from whom the book derives its title), the apocryphal *Gospel of Judas*, and other assorted ephemera. A strange mélange to be sure, and one with no claims to finality. Rather I hope that in this accrual of things which have caught my attention that some broad intimation of what goodness might mean can be approached.

It should be noted that this book was written in the autumn

of 2017, a historically tumultuous time – as they all are – though perhaps a bit more tumultuous than most. Looming over my concerns is clearly the current political climate in both Europe and the United States, particularly the increasing economic disparity, the emboldening of extremism and zealotry, and especially the casual cruelty. The desire to reflect on what goodness might mean and how to be an embodied individual implicated in systems of oppression who nonetheless wishes to stand against those systems is hopefully underscored through the entire book. It should be, it was written under the duress of Facebook notification, push notification, and viral tweet, all indicating the birth of some rough beast slouched towards some such place. And yet the names of those modern demons appear nowhere in this book. That's intentional – I've written their names enough elsewhere.

It also should be said that in many ways, though I rarely appear as a character in these observations, that this is perhaps my most personal piece of published writing. While *America and Other Fictions* bares the mark of my experience, I think that *Furnace of this World* is, to me at least, a much more obvious artifact of things I've loved, things I've lost, things I've feared, things I've prayed for. That being said, I broach very little autobiographical detail, which in all of my writing is both a function of conscious design as well as the implicit result of what I'm interested in. Christ knows I've not got the hubris to straight-face claim that I'm not a bit of a narcissist, but I do think that I've achieved the pragmatic enough realization that nobody is particularly interested in the random details of life for a rapidly aging contingent academic and freelance writer. That being said, this can't help but be the most personal of accounts (at least for me), and as a psychic map I ask you to evidence goodness in your treatment. Finally, a word of thanks must be given to editor Russell Bennetts at *Berfrois* magazine, the most innovative and adventuresome of British literary sites, where much of this material first appeared, and who has been an indefatigable advocate for allowing my sometimes-strange writings to appear for an audience in a manner that they never would normally.

Dear reader, if there is any vision I wish you to have, I would want it to be one of our system-skeptic Blake, who when he was nine viewed "a tree full of angels," and at four witnessed God putting "his head in the window." I've always been partial to the second example myself, thinking of spooky, weird, fat little baby Blake playing in his Moravian mother's kitchen, perhaps smashing a ladle upon a colander and absent-mindedly reveling in the cacophony as God strolled down the Lambeth road outside their cottage, enjoying the cool of the evening as the sun set into its orange dusk, pausing long enough to stick His big bearded wooly head in through their window and startling the young prophet with a declarative "Hey!"

Always the oddness of this anecdote appeals to me, positing theophany as not just deeply weird and otherworldly, but paradoxically also familiar and very human. Just God pulling a bit of a prank on little William Blake. I enjoy it because it strikes me as how goodness feels, when truly approached, when truly embraced, that rare, precious moment of connection, of true human empathy, of being startled by God, not knowing whether it's the divine presence or just some random person walking down the path. Wisdom is beginning to understand that they're the same thing.

I

One fourteenth-century morning in the village of Montaillou, a simple woman named Bartholomette d'Urs, who slept every evening in her bed next to her young son, awoke to find that her boy had died of some unknown cause in the night. Perhaps some infection that was impossible for the medicine of the era to identify or treat, or an accident that led to the crushing of the infant and which d'Urs was too heartbroken to confess to, or simply one of the common tragedies whereby a child dies for some unknown reason. Jacques Fournier, both the official inquisitor and the bishop whose reach included this Pyrenees town, and who would one day reign from Peter's second chair in Avignon as Pope Benedict XII, recorded Montaillou's spiritual comings and goings for 1318 through 1325. Charged with enforcing theological conformity in those years when the dualistic Cathar heresy beguiled the French people away from the certainties of the One True Church, Fournier provided a creedal biography of this community of only a few hundred endangered souls (as all souls are so endangered, of course). Fournier recorded the incident, which was later elaborated on by French historian Emmanuel Le Roy Ladurie in his 1975 *annales* microhistory *Montaillou, village occitan de 1294 à 1324*. D'Urs' unbaptized baby was officially besmirched with that original sin passed down unbroken through generations, but that poor infant must surely have seemed as innocent as the lamb to his grieving mother. Still, this unbaptized baby's ultimate destination was forever ambiguous, for he did not yet know the cleansing water of the sacrament. Perhaps he would dwell in the Arcadian hills of Limbo with Homer, Horace, Ovid, and Saladin. But d'Urs was a Catholic, and whether she was bound for hell, purgatory, or heaven was an issue of her conduct, and regardless of whether her life was faithful or not, good or not, she was guaranteed that she would never see her beloved child again, for she would never be bound for Limbo. God may have given his only living Son, but being God He at least had the certainty that He would see his boy again, d'Urs (like all of us) must live in painful ambiguity which the Lord is lucky enough to be incapable of experiencing. And so, d'Urs went to find some certainty, some supplication, and some succor from her priest. He told the woman, "Do not weep. God will give the soul of your dead son to the next child you conceive, male or female. Or else his soul will find a good home somewhere else." Such consolation, such affirmation! The vagaries of theology are what they are, guiding words at best and baroque idols at worst, but this priest embodied his pastoral role, truly a good shepherd in telling d'Urs what he did. Fournier did not agree. The priest, whose comfort to the woman sounded a bit too much like that Pythagorean metempsychosis of the Albigensian heretics still hiding as remnants in those Occitan hills, was imprisoned for heresy for eight years, and forced to forever wear the yellow cross of heresy upon his cloak. Did she find comfort in the priest's utterance? Did he ever regret telling her what he did? Was the priest a Cathar, did he genuinely believe in reincarnation? Or was his comfort just a bit of human sweetness, a sacred white lie? Maybe he was orthodox, but thought that the only soul being endangered by such a lie was his own. Does it matter? I think that he was probably a very good man.

II

Whither reincarnation, or paradise, or perdition, or salvation, or damnation? Fodder for schoolmen and philosophers, yet also visceral and tangible for the mere believer. What is truth without compassion? All the salvation d'Urs needed was perhaps in that priest's noble falsehood, and perhaps both of their souls were saved then, a moment of heaven experienced during that supposedly misguided sacrament. Religions tend to be founded by advocates for the spirit of the law, but they are normally governed by partisans of its letter. From Christ's parable of the Good Samaritan to Hillel discoursing about the Golden Rule while standing on one leg, our religious traditions emphasize that before God is one of truth, or justice, or even law, that he is a God of mercy. "Prisons are built with stones of Law," as William Blake said, and in God there can only ever be freedom. No doubt the adherent of orthodoxy, concerned as he is with correct belief, would disagree with my sentimentalizing of the Occitan priest. If it is true that correct belief is necessary to our salvation, then who am I to celebrate his indiscretion, offering d'Urs a bit of arguably illusory comfort at possibly the expense of her mortal soul? Is that not the road to theological relativism, the chicanery of a New Age gospel where feeling alright is more important than the creed? Maybe. But I don't think so.

III

Don't mistake me here – I'm not an antinomian, or at least I'm a pretty bad antinomian, and an even more boring libertine. I'm not speaking against the law *per se,* and I have no interest in ham-fisted allegories pitting obstinate, stiff-necked legalism against some sort of freeing gospel. Laws and rules are like people – good and bad. And when they serve the interests of justice, they can be very good indeed. But I do think distinction must be made between issues of ritual and metaphysics – which also like people can be good or bad – and ethics. Nothing necessarily too radical here, assuming that you're not Benedict XII doling out the yellow cross of punishment to our poor priest. But in our own era, when all epistemic certainty has been on a slow fizzle from the sixteenth-century onward, when both fideism and positivism seem like a sucker's game, you can see how some diseased minds would be attracted to certain forces of occult reaction, the "Dark Enlightenment" or whatever you call that mélange of Randian libertarianism, neo-monarchism, social Darwinism, and flat-out fedora wearing douchebaggery. The net result of that Cartesian thinking which maintains that axiomatic first principles and pure deductive reasoning can generate a complete ethical system is that sooner or later when the ladder of reason is shown to be unsteady and gets kicked over you start to get anxious that you're going to be stuck up in that tree, and then you're willing to listen to anyone who walks by and claims that they can get you down. In building an ethic from deductive axiomatic first principles, in the end, it is reason which ironically gets abandoned. Christ, I sound like Edmund Burke, don't I? Well that's embarrassing, I promise you that I mostly disagree with him. But might I suggest, that if we're to build any kind of ethic, it comes not from the first rules of the Euclidian moralizer, the Benthemite with his felicific calculus where you plug in values like "propinquity," "fecundity," and "duration" to arrive

13

at a numeric answer to what's the greatest for the greatest number; nor from the decrees of revealed religion, but rather from that shared moment of connection between individuals in pain (as all individuals are)? A connection that we've elected to call compassion? In other words, I neither know what is right or wrong, nor how to prove which one a given action is, but I do know fear, anxiety, pain, relief, peace, love, and the visceral, physical, psychological experience of those states, and that must be the basis for any ethic of goodness to our fellow humans. That's not relativism, it's an acknowledgment that empty is the ethic which theorizes first principles, but not the desire to embrace someone in pain; lame is the theology which parses rituals, but does not have an awareness that to feed the hungry and heal the suffering is the aim of faith; sophistic is the philosophy which explicates the epistemology of morality, but does not give a dollar to the homeless guy standing outside of Penn Station. And lest you think me preachy, I'll cop to only walking quicker past those guys as well. If humans were angels there would be no need of rules, and all the rest, but humans are humans and that should be good enough to build a moral of feeling, and an ethic of empathy. Do you feed the hungry because Christ says you should, or because rational first principles say that feeding the hungry maximizes overall order in the world, or conversely do you not feed the hungry because you're an everyman-for-himself type who quotes Austrian economists? No, you feed the hungry because you have a stomach – and that's where morality has to begin, not in our heads, or even our hearts, but our bowls and bowels. Why the skepticism about doing what's right, or being able to justify it by recourse to some absolute quality, whether God or reason? You try to do good because you're a person in the world and people should try to do what's good. Tautological? Very well then. Doesn't alter the reality that goodness isn't about what's argued for in the *Metaphysics of Morals*, or certainly with what's contained in Leviticus, or even in the Sermon on the Mount, but that goodness is about holding another's hand in the dark so that you're both a little less frightened about the fact that you will one day die. If the rules help in that endeavor then great, and if not, then hold high that value which states that kindness is always the only rule that really matters. Goodness is never circumscribed by law, or literalism, or mere metaphysical speculation, it is only defined by compassion. So that's the first axiom.

IV

God in the earliest pages of the Torah is a tangible deity, who for all of his abstractions (rarely is he ever literally described) is still identifiably corporeal, enjoying as he does a quiet walk through the cooling of the evening as the first dusk's spindly orange fingers close on the glowing western horizon. If he is ineffable to us then he seems frankly present to the patriarchs, if a bit mysterious, if not a bit spooky. Think of God and his two strange compatriots (angels? Persons of the Trinity?), dining in a sandy tent with Abraham upon that Jordanian plain, supping on what, lentils and flat-bread? Chickpeas and figs? I imagine it as a silent dinner, until those negotiations where the ever-faithful Abraham tried to intervene on behalf of the people of Sodom, including his nephew Lot – for if the Bible is anything it's an account of how one must always be willing to negotiate with an unpredictable being such as God. The Lord assured Abraham that Sodom would be spared from destruction if fifty righteous people who dwelled within that city could be found. How about forty-five? Forty? Thirty? Surely twenty? What about ten people? If ten righteous men were found would that be enough to off-set the iniquity and sin of the other multitude in that malevolent twinned city? And so a deal was struck, and the angels were dispatched to discover if any light, any benevolence hid among that wicked assemblage. To spare you the suspense, they would discover only one supposedly good man in the entire town. As they found it, that would be Lot himself, a man who apparently evidenced more goodness than all the other inhabitants of that place. Lot, a man who was good enough to protect his angelic guests from being raped by a crowd of Sodom's citizens who were at his door, but who was also the man who proffered as a solution letting those same Sodomites rape his daughters instead. The same daughters whom he would later have sex with in a cave overlooking the burnt remains of the city. That – that

16

was the best man in Sodom. I am not being sarcastic. Who are we to say that such a man, who by any standard of decency would certainly be considered despicable today, didn't evidence just enough righteousness that he should have his own soul sparred, if not that of the rest of Sodom? Goodness has to work with what it has, I guess.

V

Lot's being the spared person among a group of unrepentant sinners is not the first instance of God's magnanimity in the Bible; there is of course Noah's exemption from the deluge earlier in the Genesis narrative. The account of Sodom and Gomorrah has an additional element however, and that is Abraham's strange negotiation with the Lord, bargaining for the survival of the former city if a certain minimum threshold of good individuals could be found. Noah's world was presumably screwed from the get-go, since as righteous as Noah may have been it seemingly never occurred to him to haggle over its continued survival if good men and women other than his family members could be found in that otherwise sin-filled antediluvian age. We encounter a strange and fascinating idea in Abraham's attempt to spare all the inhabitants of Sodom – righteous and unrighteous alike – based on the presence of some specific number of good people. Genesis implies that the mere existence of goodness at a certain critical level is enough to redeem the rest of us. Sodom is composed of almost entirely sinners, and based on a reading of the text itself, in opposition to the common definition of "Sodomy" today, it seems that the ancient Sodomites were primarily guilty of rape, rejection of the stranger, and greed, which might as well be the platform of one of the United States' major political parties in 2020. Abraham's is an evocative suggestion – could the presence of righteous, good individuals compensate for all of the rest of that evil? And what is an equivalent amount of absolute good when weighed against absolute evil? Good seems to sell at a much higher level than does evil; even factoring the presumed smallness of Bronze Age cities in Canaan, one would imagine that Abraham's initial proposal of the discovery of fifty righteous people being able to justify sparing the entire city would still be a relatively small percentage of Sodom (the population of that village wasn't fifty-one). Demographers put the average size of the major Middle Eastern communities in the second millennium of the common era (when it's presumed that the patriarchal age of the Bible is set) at anywhere from 10,000 to the veritable Times Square that is bustling Uruk at 80,000 souls. In either case, fifty is a relatively small percentage to off-set all of that iniquity from everyone else, and of course even smaller is forty-five, thirty, twenty, or ten. Typologically the narrative prefigures Christ's sacrifice, where one righteous man can compensate for everything else wicked that the rest of us are engaged with. As it was, Abraham's proposal could never be tested, since ten good men couldn't be found in all of Sodom. It's too bad he didn't negotiate the deal down to one person.

VI

One would, of course, be an auspicious number, not least of which because it's the smallest number of people you can have around while still having people around (or person around, if we're being grammatically correct). Don't sell ten short though, there is a lot of numerological significance to the number ten (though of course the number forty, Abraham's starting point in the divine deal-making, is similarly important). The ancient Hebrews, like the Romans, counted in a base ten numeric system, but beyond the mathematical importance of the number, it's also repeated throughout the Tanakh. There are, after all, ten plagues which bedevil the Egyptians, ten days between Rosh Hashanah and Yom Kippur, and ultimately ten lost tribes of Israel after that northern kingdom is run over by the Assyrians. And, of course, there are Ten Commandments, even if Jews, Catholics, Orthodox, and Protestants disagree on how to group those decrees in Exodus. But ritually, the number ten is most important in Jewish practice in terms of the *minyan*. Certain prayers, in particular public ones, can only occur within the context of the community, and both the Palestinian and the Babylonian Talmud agree that the minimum number of Jews needed to fulfill the quorum of the minyan is ten. The connection to Abraham's and God's final agreed upon amount for the minimum number of righteous Sodomites needed to spare that city seem obvious, almost as if the presence of a minyan of ten praying Jews fulfills a similar role of supplication in any subsequent age (and to thus presumably avoid apocalyptic disaster). Easy to assume, but not the actual logic used in either version of the Talmud. The authoritative Babylonian Talmud, in Megillah 23b, justifies the number of a minyan being as based on three different scriptural sources, none of which involved Abraham and Sodom (for you *Inside Baseball* types, the Babylonian Talmud cites a verse in Leviticus and two in Numbers in justifying the quorum number). The earlier

Jerusalem Talmud does cite Genesis in its justification for the number ten (along with three other scriptural references), but the derivation from Genesis is at 42:5, in a portion of the Joseph story, again having nothing to do with that forlorn undiscovered party of ten on a hot and rainy day in old Sodom. But the resonance seems unmistakable, that there is some minimum number of the good, some smallest amount of goodness, that though it be tiny is still fierce, that despite being miniscule, could still have the power to save the world. That evil might be massive, that its tendrils may fill and flit into every corner of the world like the brimstone and smoke of burning Sodom covering the doorways and alleys and creeping down the stone roads, but that despite evil's seeming all-encompassing power, it can be defeated with just an atom of goodness.

VII

Seven is also an integer of numerological significance, whose entry in the encyclopedia of gematria would be longer than average. And thus, observation seven is more than an appropriate place to discuss another religiously weighty number: 36.. That particular number is important to this idea of there being a minimum number of good people required to stave off apocalyptic destruction. The Talmud, at both Tractate Sanhedrin 97b and Tractate Sukha 45b, speaks of a class of human being known as the *Tzadkhim Nistarim,* the "hidden righteous ones," sometimes also referred to as the *Lamed vav Tzadkhim,* or the "thirty-six righteous ones." Lamed vav Tzadkhim are among those esoteric and frankly weird ideas that sprinkle the ephemera of organized faith, an idea that for all of its strangeness contains a fundamental wisdom, albeit in enigmatic form. As a concept it posits that at any given moment in human history, whether we speak of the era of Abraham, or that of Christ, or Luther, or Lincoln, or us, that there are exactly 36 hidden, purely righteous men and women whose continued existence is that upon which the rest of ours' hinges. This quorum of the absolutely good are all that stand between the rest of us sinners and the world's destruction, they provide enough cumulative goodness that they pull the rest of us along with them, their righteousness constitutes those kernels of dispersed resistance against the entropy of evil, the machinations of malice. They are as a stop in the door of reality, wedging the entrance open just enough so that the light can continue to come in. Among the 36 humans there will be a range of ages, from newborn mewling infants, to crooked dying old men; when one expires, another is born. A member of the 36 can live in any country and on any continent, they can be rich or poor, smart or stupid, beautiful or ugly. Anyone you've met, anyone you walk past on a busy Manhattan street, or in a small Illinois town, or at a midnight diner, or on a Greyhound bus, could be one of them. The *lamed vovnicks* (as they're called in Yiddish) don't know each other, and in fact they are unaware of their own status as being members of such a crucial minority. If somebody claims to be a lamed vovnick then it is most certainly instant assurance that they are not one, for the humility of such a saint necessitates that they themselves are incapable of conceiving of their own self-identity in such grandiose terms. I say that despite the strangeness of its literalism (where the hell do those ancient sages get the number 36?), which leaves open the question of whether it is description or allegory, the concept does serve the rhetorical function that the best of parables share. The idea of the lamed vovnick reminds us of two things: that goodness can be obscured and hidden within our midst, and that even the smallest of victories for goodness is as a complete triumph when it is viewed through the totalizing hungry eyes of absolute Evil, who can broach absolutely no defeat, even of the smallest kind. From among their ranks, in every generation, comes the potential anointed one, the *moshiach*, the messiah; though, like the hidden Mahdi, they will only arrive when either the world is so full of goodness that they can safely and easily be revealed, or conversely when everything is so degraded, wicked, awful, and evil that they have no choice but to be revealed so as to save us. As the German Jewish philosopher (and kabbalah enthusiast) Walter Benjamin put it in his 1940 essay *Theses on the Philosophy of History,* "For every second of time was the strait gate through which the Messiah might enter." Every hour, minute, and second is a portal through which the *moshiach* may arrive, and though the admixture ratio of goodness to wickedness may shift throughout the ages of humanity, those stalwart, absolute 36 unknown to each other or themselves forever stand guard against our complete inundation by evil. Recalling those Hasidic folktales which imagine an immortal Elijah covered in sores and swaddled in rags, his identity hidden to everyone, wandering through the frozen paths of Poland and Ukraine's shtetls, trying to find some succor, or of Christ hidden as a beggar. And anyone could theoretically be a member of this group, perhaps you, perhaps me (but probably not). Possibly the tired but cheerful barista who gave you back your incorrect change, the kid selling candy-bars for his school at rush-hour on the Q train, the woman begging in front of a Midtown skyscraper, with so many acid burns on her face that you have to avert your eyes, because her deformity sickens your stomach.

VIII

By one of those rhetorically convenient coincidences that are ever-useful to writers such as myself, but which may or may not have any actual significance in their own right, the number 36 appears in a source very different from the Talmud. In 1895, Rhode Island born French writer Georges Polti published an unusual little book entitled *Les trente-six situations dramatiques,* one of those periodic texts in which the author claims to have identified the minimum number of possible narrative plots across novels, drama, and epic (and perhaps presumably life as well, however we choose to organize the order of those events). From Vladimir Propp's Russian formalist *The Morphology of the Folktale* (with its almost mathematical short-hand for folkloric narrative tropes including "RECEIPT OF A MAGICAL AGENT" and "WEDDING") to Christopher Booker's Jungian archetype inflected *The Seven Basic Plots,* or the Aarne-Thompson Classification Index, the Arthurian Grail (there's a plot!) of narratology has been the proper identification and organization of the basic elements of any story that we could tell. And, over a pint, you'll hear all sorts of numbers bandied about, from Booker's seven to Polti's 36. Kurt Vonnegut thought that there were six and John Gardner thought that there were only two (somebody goes on a journey, a stranger comes to town). Polti's system of categorization is more baroque than most, but for my purposes it has the nice resonance of listing a number of plots equivalent to the number of unseen lamed vovnicks in the world. From the first plot ("The supplicant appeals to the power in authority for deliverance from the persecutor") to the thirty-sixth ("The killing of the Kinsman Slain by the Executioner is witnessed by the Kinsman") Polti argued that he had discovered a classification system whereby every story that had or could be told had been properly identified. His system does seem thorough, running through comedy and tragedy, transcendent of mere genre or mode, encompassing the grand narrative threads of humanity in all of its complexity. Consider situation number three, "Crime pursued by vengeance," where "The criminal commits a crime that will not see justice, so the avenger seeks justice by punishing the criminal," or situation thirty-one which sees "Conflict with a god." I like to think that each one of Polti's dramatic scenarios corresponds exactly to the life-stories of all of those lamed vovnicks living in our midst. Maybe the previously mentioned first plot corresponds to that hidden lamed vovnick who is an overworked public defender working hard to have a woman's wrongly imprisoned son released? Maybe situation two ("Deliverance") corresponds to the woman who jumps onto the train tracks to save a child who has fallen onto the platform? If each one of Polti's scenarios corresponded to the individual tales of those hidden righteous it would underscore the diversity of goodness, how it manifests itself, the variety of people and situations in which goodness can be found. What Elijah in shadows or Christ obscured teach us is not that we should treat all of our fellow humans with compassion because they might secretly be Elijah or Christ, but rather that all of our fellow humans, in a manner, actually already are Elijah and Christ, regardless of where their tab is set for the moral goodness account. Who knows what benevolence beats in the heart of the sinner, for Christ was strung up between two criminals. So, let it not be lost that not all of the plots are ones which necessarily reflect positively on their protagonist, because that's precisely the point. It's hard to see the goodness implicit in situation three's revenger, or the main character in situation thirteen ("Enmity of Kin") as being a saint – but maybe that's the point. After all, we're speaking of the 36 lamed vovnicks, not saints. Again, goodness has to work with what it has.

IX

Augustine famously posited that evil was not a positive category, rather it was simply the absence of the good. Maybe he had that reversed, maybe good is simply the absence of evil? But that doesn't sound right, does it? If evil has a visceral, tangible, physical reality, one that you can identify emotionally in its presence, the feeling of a cool, calm, intentional, smirking *something* behind the veil of everyday reality, of creatures that make your scalp shrink and the hair on your arms stand erect, and of a *something* whose designs we see in whatever atrocities we occasion upon, from the twisted accounts of concentration camp guards and serial killers, then good must of course also be similarly positive and tangible in its existence. And, as evil has that physical effect on us, so must the presence of the actual, glowing, touched *Good*. From stories of anonymous self-sacrifice, of tenderness, compassion, empathy, then goodness seems like a real *thing* just as surely as evil does – a self-evident truth observed by the very fact of being alive for a little bit among our individual little plots of land. If Augustine saw good as total and evil as mainly a matter of perspective, then the prophet Mani (of whom Augustine was a follower in his youth) rather borrowed from Persian Zoroastrianism and preached that the universe is forever locked in a state of permanent combat from roughly equally powerful absolute Good and Evil. You get no opinions from me on the accuracy of either model, I'm not in the theodicy business here. Rather, what I offer is a simple vision, and you can draw whatever philosophical conclusions from it that you wish. Imagine a cloudless ink-black night sky on some hypothetical world with a variable number of stars. There could be so many stars that the entire night sky is transformed into a blazing world of glorious light, or there can be only one star, but there can never be less than that. But even if there is only one star in that night sky, it's still enough to make out the human face of the person next to you on the surface of that otherwise dark planet.

X

That speaks to the nature of absolute evil – its psychology is totalizing, it requires nothing less than complete dominance, total control over everything. Anything less than totality is a defeat for absolute evil, for the capricious, cannibalistic, carnivorous hunger of evil allows only for the devouring of everything. Evil is by its nature a beast of avarice. So to prevent evil's victory at the level of a mile, a foot, an inch, and for just a day, an hour, or a second might seem as if a small victory on behalf of goodness, but for absolute evil the existence or endurance of any goodness is a total failure, for the greediness of absolute malice abides by no partial victories. This is the second axiom, and it can be referred to as the "non-totalizing power of goodness." If anything, goodness is good not in spite of its modest non-totalizing, but in part because of it.

XI

Pray that in the last moments before his execution at the Flossenbürg concentration camp that Dietrich Bonhoeffer was able to call into his memory some of those black gospel songs which he loved so much. That in the minutes and seconds before he would be lynched by the Nazis that he was able to perhaps remember the melodies of Thomas Dorsey, Sallie Martin, Mahalia Jackson, or Sister Rosetta Tharpe and that he drew some of that sweet comfort which sings that there "will be peace in the valley for me, some day." Consider Bonhoeffer – the slight, anxious, bookish, effeminate, and incomparably brave man who would be martyred in that factory of death. When Bonhoeffer studied towards his Doctor of Theology degree at the University of Berlin, religion was arguably more academic than personal for him, more a set of interesting cultural and intellectual propositions than a living gospel. Born in a largely secular family enraptured to Enlightenment ideals, religion was more puzzle than guide, something approached with the head before the heart. In 1930, when he had the opportunity to continue his studies at Union Theological Seminary in New York, he embarked to the New World with little enthusiasm. Of America, he wrote, "There is no theology here." What theological brilliance could there be in America, a land of holly rollers and snake oil salesman, given over to the empty enthusiasms of revival and faith healers, a land that hadn't produced a bona fide theological genius since Jonathan Edwards? And yet there was a genius in American religion which Bonhoeffer encountered after his new friend and fellow seminarian Frank Fisher encouraged the young German academic to venture further uptown. It was at Harlem's Abyssinian Baptist Church at the heights of the Depression and three years before Hitler would come to power that Bonhoeffer first encountered the living God, the God of the oppressed, the God who had stood before Pharaoh. Listening to the Revered

Adam Clayton Powell Sr., Bonhoeffer didn't necessarily learn anything he hadn't already known, but he finally understood it. Raised on the neoclassical perfections of Bach and Mendelsohn, the Romantic pathos of Beethoven and Schubert, he had never quite heard anything like the Negro spiritual. Bonhoeffer was so taken with the Abyssinian Baptist Church that he became a Sunday school teacher there, the quiet German making his way from the Upper West Side to Harlem every weekend. The Bible, of course, was used as a means of oppression against slaves who were wretched across the Earth on the teeming hell-scape factories that were the boats of the Middle Passage. From the hermeneutic of oppression came ignoble lies like the Curse of Ham, or the platitudes of Paul imploring the slave to cheerfully serve his master. And, the Bible, of course, was also used as a potent means of resistance, the cry of "Let my people go" beginning first as whisper, repeating as *idee fix*, and concluding as triumphant declaration. The example of the slave rebellion leader Nat Turner demonstrates both contradictory observations. Now, here in the Abyssinian Baptist Church, the descendants of those slaves brought to bear the accumulated religious wisdom of how faith operates, and how it is necessary, when the boot of oppression is pressing on your neck. Slaves, prohibited from reading by their masters, would meet by moonlight to study the Bible, its stories of Pharaoh and Nebuchadnezzar and Haman humbled before the Lord, for God was not of the masters, but of the servants. Those nocturnal, clandestine gatherings of Christ – those churches – evoked nothing so much as the first generations of Christians meeting in subterranean Roman catacombs. And as it would be, they prefigured Bonhoeffer's own Confessing Church, formed in the decade after he returned from Harlem to the Babylon that was Nazi Germany. A gathering of Protestant clergy who rejected the idolatries of so-called "Aryan Christianity" where Constantine's cross was beaten into Hitler's sword. From Rev Powell, Bonhoeffer understood that "the Black Christ is preached with rapturous passion and vision," that Christ is always black, and a Jew, and a Gypsy, and anyone who is ever the dispossessed of the world. But Christians, like any group of people, are often more than willing to deny the savior before the cock has even crowed, so as to gain a little security or power. Many Christians in Bonhoeffer's Germany gladly welcomed this Hitler who would have sent the Lord to the gas chamber. And so, the Nazis founded a heretical German Evangelical Church, which was to subsume all of the Protestant denominations of the country under a new doctrine which denied Christ's Judaism and purged the scripture of the Old Testament. In response, men like Karl Barth, Bonhoeffer, and many of the remainder of the pious resistance of Germany formed the underground Confessing Church to act in opposition to Hitler, not just spiritually but in providing material means of escape for Jews and other persecuted minorities. In that later role, Bonhoeffer was recruited by his brother-in-law Hans von Dohnányi into one of the German government's intelligence rings, the Abwehr, to act as a double-agent. Under the guise of his ecumenical connections around the world being helpful to the Reich, Bonhoeffer and Dohnányi delivered information from the anti-Nazi resistance to contacts in western intelligence agencies. And so, the tweedy theologian more conversant with Augustine, Luther, and Calvin than with cryptography, subterfuge, and drop-off boxes was suddenly a spy against *Der Fuhrer*. While in this service, Bonhoeffer learned from Dohnányi, who was involved, that there was a plot to assassinate Hitler being hatched within the Abwehr. As a committed Christian, Bonhoeffer understood that for all of Hitler's wickedness, he was still a man, created in the image of God as all men are. And, as a committed Christian and pacifist, Bonhoeffer understood that to take a life – any life – is a grave sin. To do so is to destroy a world, for the commandment to not murder has no asterisks by it. And yet as a human being he also knew that despite those theological abstractions that it was morally and ethically just and imperative that Adolf Hitler must be killed. So Bonhoeffer, the Christian and pacifist, aided in whatever way he could to make sure that that result came to pass. And for that he and his brother-in-law were arrested on April 5, 1943, beginning two years of imprisonment and torture before his execution. Of the brilliant theologians that the twentieth-century produced – Karl Barth, Paul Tillich, Reinhold Niebuhr, Hans Kung – there are many who have earned our respect, because of their erudition, their learnedness, and yes, their humanity. Yet among all of them it is only Bonhoeffer whom it is easy to love, for he was willing to make that supreme sacrifice of his own deeply felt principles so as to lead to a greater good, even if he would risk damnation to do it. As he wrote, "when a man takes guilt upon himself in responsibility, he imputes his guilt to himself and no one else. He answers for it…Before other men he is justified by dire necessity; before himself he is acquitted by his conscience, but before God he hopes only for grace." In Bonhoeffer's harrowing of hell he risked his own damnation so as to save others. He died two weeks before the 90th and 97th United States Army divisions liberated Flossenbürg. Pray that he had music in his heart, for he was a supremely good man.

XII

Sometimes goodness is expressed with denying official teaching, as with our Occitan priest, and sometimes goodness is manifested by denying God's commandments, as with our German theologian. Let's make that the third axiom. That will be the terms of the conversation.

XIII

Blessed is he among all the saints, for spurned though he is, Judas Iscariot was the one who first set the world towards its redemption, with a kiss. For that loyalty to God, Christ was resurrected, but lamentable Judas must forever sit in the frozen mouth of Satan, unfairly locked in icy embrace with other traitors. Slavoj Žižek has written that "Judas' act of betrayal was the highest sacrifice, the ultimate fidelity." Sacrilegious? Blasphemous? Heretical? Such a conclusion is the logical result of Christianity itself. If Christ's death upon the cross redeemed the world, then it was only Judas' betrayal of Christ which facilitated that grace. Consider it: we're told that God so loved the world that He gave His only Son to die for our sins. As extreme as such a moment of pain must be – the scouring and whipping, the bloody perforated wrists, the breath crushed out of collapsing lungs – the experience was also finite. Most deaths are easier than crucifixion, though not all deaths. And hell is harder than any death. The nature of Christ's sacrifice lay in the humbled indignity of the Ultimate dying upon the cross, but then surely any manner of death would be indignity enough to redeem creation? Did Christ's blood spilled upon Golgotha's rock have to come from the cat-o-nines and nails, or could it have been equally capable of saving us if spilled silently within an artery of his brain as he died a peaceful death as some forgotten old man? Apparently not, apparently it was upon that hill that He was supposed to die. We can debate the soteriological specifics of Christ's redemptive death, but that Judas' betrayal must be the ultimate sacrifice seems unassailable to me, the necessary conclusion drawn from the story's logic. Of the two, Christ spent three days in hell, but Judas has to spend an eternity there. Might it be as appropriate to say that Judas died for your sins – still dies for all of our sins? Christ supposedly sits at the right-hand of God, neighbor to his Father in the judgment of all of humanity. And where is Judas? In hell, perhaps boiling in a massive pot of semen and excrement, forced to fry in an unholy oil of that which life comes from and that from which it must ever return, a disgraceful punishment for a man for whom we indirectly owe our salvation. To burn forever in hell, for all of us? Can you imagine a greater sacrifice? Can you envision anyone more good than that?

XIV

Look upon that blessed face. There are so many Judases, there is he of the reptilian sneer and the hooked nose slithering up to his kiss with Christ, there is the dignified rebel who fought Roman domination, there is the ever-faithful right-hand man. For so few lines in the Bible being devoted to the red-headed zealot, he haunts our culture as surely as the Wandering Jew Ahasver perambulates around the globe. Examine Giotto di Bondone's depiction of the kiss of Judas, as painted inside a Padua chapel in the early fourteenth century, and still visible there today. Characteristic of Giotto's style, and reflective of the increasing realism of late medieval art, Giotto presents a chaotic tableaux *in media res*. Judas and Jesus are framed by disciples fighting centurions; at the left edge of the fresco, Peter seems to be in the process of losing his ear. Torches and clubs are raised. At the center, an unsteady, uncertain, uncomfortable Judas embraces a golden haloed Christ. Theirs is a seemingly silent, personal, private moment amid the rest of the cacophony, a quiet cell, a subatomic particle of connection at the center of history commencing around them. A strikingly personal moment, there amid the violence of the rest of the scene. The two men share an unmistakably charged interaction, for there is often nothing more intimate than a kiss. Yes, Judas wears his characteristic yellow robe, which for medieval viewers would indelibly signal his Jewishness (as Jews of the period were often forced to wear a yellow badge, solidifying their connection to gold in the minds of medieval bigots). And yes, Judas' curly hair marks him as Semitic, even as Christians often conveniently forget Jesus' ethnicity. But look closer, this painting isn't a typical hatchet job. Judas steadies himself at a distance, not totally committed to the betrayal which redemption depends on. And his face – it is not exactly the face of a man who is confident in the rightness of his chosen (or commanded?) course. It is pained, uncertain.

It is arguably the face of a man who is angry, heartbroken; a man who has already been betrayed in a manner too intimate for him to ever be able to describe to us. There is a gap between Judas and Jesus; their lips have either just touched, or are about too. And in that distance between the two there is the infinite enormity which constitutes the definition of humanity, for we all live in that space. Malicious betrayal, or commanded loyalty? Here is the crux: when it comes to Judas' goodness or perfidy, both are accurate explanations of the thirteenth disciple, even in their contradictions. Especially in them. Betrayal of the Lord isn't incidental – it's the whole point. It's why there has to be a savior in the first place. It's that which justifies Judas' counterintuitive goodness. Jesus tells his friend in Nikos Kazantzakis' sublime *The Last Temptation of Christ* that "God pitied me and gave me the easier task: to be crucified," for it's the betrayal which is the real sacrifice. Everyone's face is the face of Judas, for we are all Judas. Whether good or evil, monstrous or human, it's all of us kissing the savior, and because of that we're all the more in need of that kiss. Christianity's fullest explication, when the Bible is read correctly (in the diabolical sense) is that we're all christs as well – goodness and evil intimately twinned together, being capable of both everything good and of a deep wickedness, sometimes in the space of but a few minutes. Nikos Kazantzakis' Jesus in *The Last Temptation of Christ* says to Judas, "We two must save the world. Help me." And so it remains.

XV

For twenty centuries of stony nightmare, it was the Judas of the passion play who was the inspiration for otherwise good Christians to slit the throats of their Jewish neighbors, to burn their synagogues, and to tear their Torahs. Judas may have been responsible for the death of one Jew, but it was the followers of that executed Jew who have been responsible for the deaths of millions of his brothers and sisters. Persecution, pogrom, genocide, Holocaust – these are the undeniable legacies of the deep metaphysic of anti-Semitism which is threaded through the Passion narrative like so much rot that can't yet be separated from healthy wood. Judas – he who is spurned, spat at, persecuted, hated, and killed. If the lamb takes the iniquity of mankind upon himself it's hard not to see Judas as being the true light unto the nations. The messiah is by his (or her) very nature one who must be spat on and spurned. There is no triumphant parade leading into Jerusalem, only those following an old, mangy ass. A messiah who isn't dejected can be no messiah at all. As orthodox a theologian as Karl Barth wrote that "Judas is the most important figure in the New Testament apart from Jesus... For he, and he alone of the apostles, was actively at work... in the accomplishment of what was God's will and what became the content of the Gospel. Yet he is the very one who is most explicitly condemned by the Law of God." How much more dejected can a messiah be than to be an invisible messiah? The recognized messiah is a limited messiah, it's only in rejection that He can truly fulfill His promise. Judas must always be a Jew; as Christ must always be a Jew. Judas must always be black; as Christ must always be black. The Devil is always a white man, respectable in his carriage, but all of our saviors – Christ and His betrayer alike – must be from among the dispossessed. Countee Cullen understood that, writing from those frantic, neon streets of Harlem in the 1920s, while reflecting on the similarities of both Christ on his cross and lynched Judas hanging above Judean sands. Twinned deaths that bore an iconographic similarity to America's indigenous strange fruit. From Golgotha, from Akeldama, from the blood-soaked potter's fields of a thousand sites of execution across the United States – Cullen asked how such sacrifice could save anybody? Lord, forgive them – if You can – for they know not what they do. The bulging eyes and swollen empurpled tongue, the charred flesh, the indignity of mutilation was all on the body of Christ, and of Judas too. Cullen sang a song of a black Christ, and prayed a prayer of a black Judas too, for the central cosmic drama of sin and redemption must by necessity occur in shadows. In a 1925 ballad, he writes "Christ spoke to him with words of fire,/ 'Then, Judas, you must kill/One who you love, One who loves you/As only God's son can/This is the work for you to do/To save the creature man.'" Judas' tragedy, the tragedy of all of those spurned in God's name but who are the Lord's most faithful adherents, is that the kiss "broke his heart,/But no one knew or heard."

XVI

If my theology seems a little odd, a little off, a little slant, it really shouldn't. At least not entirely. Literary critic Susan Gubar describes the most spurned apostle as a "divine agent facilitating the resurrection of God's Son and the salvation of humanity." She explains that "The ascetic Judas mortifies not his flesh but his spirit through his immovable hostility toward grace: he renounces 'the kingdom of heaven.'" But it is only in Judas' personal renouncement of that kingdom that Peter was able to acquire those keys, so that the rest of us might be able to get in. Theology might be clear, but scripture never is. Who exactly is making the ultimate sacrifice in that narrative? Who exactly is the scapegoat? Who exactly so loved the world that he sacrificed his own eternal soul so that others may acquire life? Far from being heretical in its depictions, the Jesus in Kazantzakis' *The Last Temptation of Christ* (as well as in Martin Scorsese's film adaptation) starkly embodies orthodoxy in all of its paradoxical beauty. Christ tells His reluctant betrayer, "You are the strongest of all the companions. Only you, I think, will be able to bear it." For the Danish theologian Nils Runeberg, a fictional invention of the Argentinian master Jorge Louis Borges, there is no ambiguity in the savior's name – it is Judas. Borges, in his 1944 story *Three Versions of Judas*, presents an account of the ill-fated Runeberg, whose very name conjures nothing so much as negation. A characteristically morose Scandinavian, Runeberg ruminates on Judas across two hefty volumes of systematic theology before coming to his ultimate conclusion in 1909's *Den hemlige Frälsaren*. Before the release of his final and most controversial volume, Runeberg had already argued that "The ascetic, for the greater glory of God, degrades and mortifies the flesh; Judas did the same with the spirit." Runeberg, during his own dark night of the soul, writes that Judas "thought that happiness, like good, is a divine attribute and not to be usurped by men." The heretical theologian concludes that:

> God became a man completely, a man to the point of infamy, a man to the point of being reprehensible – all the way to the abyss. In order to save us, He could have chosen any of the destinies which together weave the uncertain web of history; He could have been Alexander, or Pythagoras, or Rurik, or Jesus; He chose an infamous destiny: He was Judas.

I've already argued, or at least entertained, much the same; though I pray that I will hopefully not have the same destitute end as Borges' invented theologian, dying broken and destitute.

XVII

Romantic Judas is a popular subject for the artist, who of course can't help but see a bit of himself (or herself) in Judas. A variety of Lord Byron, a Miltonic Lucifer standing opposed to old Nobodaddy, offering not salvation but much more potent liberation. Thomas De Quincey, that old lotus-eater, between opium puffs and laudanum sips, remarked that, "As regards the worldly prospects of this scheme, it is by no means improbable that Iscariot was right." Judas has always been a bit Romantic, a bit punk rock. Borges' Judas may be the most radical version, but Judas the Redeemable haunts even pop culture. Listen to Andrew Lloyd Webber and Tim Rice's (underrated) 1970 rock musical *Jesus Christ Superstar*. My God what a subversive masterpiece! And now they perform it in church pageants! Do these people not read the lyrics? Webber's Judas is a counter-cultural revolutionary, a Zealot who abandoned militancy in favor of spiritual rebellion, only to ultimately fear that such rebellion is ultimately toothless. Judas is a wounded idealist, the type of cynic who can only be born from a repeatedly broken heart, while Jesus is depicted as a self-serving cult leader, if ultimately still the Son of God. The hero of the play is witty, rambunctious, principled Judas. But that he must be condemned for what he has done is non-negotiable, forcing audiences shelling out for middle-brow theater to confront the most distilled of theodicies. Judas shrieks, "My mind is darkness now. My God, I'm sick. I've been used, and you knew, all the time. God, I'll never ever know why you chose me for your crime, your foul, bloody crime. You have murdered me." Poor Judas, used as a useful tool in the salvation of all of us, but cursed to never take part in the very redemption which he assured. All seems very unfair. Acknowledging that iniquity wasn't first the provenance of a hippie musical, or a blind Argentinian genius, or a piously heretical Greek novelist and his Italian-American protégée. No, the whispers of Judas' condemnation come from the very sunbaked sands of the lands where his and Jesus' story were first recorded into fraying papyrus codices.

XVIII

That Judas may have had God on his side goes back to the very beginning of the story, to when it was first told. Irenaeus, the second century Church Father and greatest of all heresiologists, considered a group known as the Cainites. These possibly apocryphal Gnostics saw God's left-hand path as the proper and (un)righteous one, preaching and living an anti-gospel. Transcendence, you see, requires transgression. In *Against Heresies*, the good Catholic Irenaeus enumerates the sins of practice these Cainites were guilty of. As if repeating one of the Proverbs of Hell, an initiate into the occult theology must maintain that "men cannot be saved until they have gone through all kinds of experience," a counter-cultural proposition which is horrifying in its implications (if fully thought out). Etymologically their strange name derives from their claimed spiritual lineage, whereby the first murderer Cain drew "his being from the Power above" and his followers thus "acknowledge that Esau, Korah, the Sodomites, and all such persons, are related to themselves." Irenaeus explains that "They declare that Judas the traitor was thoroughly acquainted with these things, and that he alone, knowing the truth as no others did, accomplished the mystery of the betrayal; by him all things, both earthly and heavenly, were thus thrown into confusion." Irenaeus assured us that such heretics drank blood and devoured flesh. That orthodoxy and heresy can so fully echo need not be a hypocrisy, but perhaps precisely the point. Irenaeus records that they ape scripture, having produced "a fictitious history of this kind, which they style the Gospel of Judas." Whether the Cainites were real or not (considering that their exploits served Irenaeus' orthodox purposes rather well), their gospel, as was discovered recently, was very real. Moldering in an Egyptian attic, the real Gospel of Judas was discovered in Beni Masar in the early 70s, right around the time that Broadway audiences were singing along to

Heaven on their Minds. Called the Codex Tchacos after the book dealer responsible for its safe-keeping, the lost gospel bounced around the antiquities market for decades, ever deteriorating, until it was translated from old Coptic by an international team in 2006 and released by the National Geographic Society. For a non-specialist, a full reading of the translated text shows a scripture that is more lacuna than writ. The cosmology is inscrutable, standard gnostic stuff about a corrupt demiurge, with guest appearances from demonic creator gods with names like Yaldabaoth and Saklas. We're informed of a place called "the immortal realm of Barbelo." The whole thing is very weird. Contrary to the breathless media-reports which implied that a reading would forever alter a Christian's relationship to their faith, the ancient manuscript is confusing, baroque, hermetic, and strange. But in its overall thrust it confirms something which Kazantzakis, Borges, Webber, Cullen, and all the rest somehow inferred on their own – that Judas was always the hero. Before the betrayal, the divine being of light who is Christ grants Judas an ascension to that realm of Barbelo above, where "Judas lifted up his eyes and saw the luminous cloud, and he entered it." Christ said unto Judas, "Lift up your eyes and look at the cloud and the light within it and the stars surrounding it. The star that leads the way is your star." His soul saw the realm of things eternal and unutterable, and as a result no man could hurt him now. And so he was free to do that which was required, to enact the saving betrayal of Christ. With almost Hemingway-like minimalism, the author of the gospel informs us that the Temple guards "approached Judas and said to him, 'What are you doing here? You are Jesus' disciple.' Judas answered them as they wished. And he received some money and handed him over to them."

XIX

Does his intent matter? It's not a small question; differences over faith and works, intent and outcome, are at the core of Christian theology. When Matthew writes of Judas that "it had been good for that man if he had not been born" that has to be literally wrong, for if Judas had never been born how would Christ's crucifixion have happened? Still, if we can agree that the results of Judas' action were ultimately good, that of course doesn't necessarily make Judas good – that's the intentionality thing. In evaluating the weight of the man's soul, it does make a difference whether he was privy to the plan and acting on Christ's accord, or if he just wanted the thirty pieces of silver. If one exonerates someone's intent because the outcome is good, we risk a type of gentle nihilism, veering into the cloying vanilla of that proclamation which has it that "God must always have a plan," as if the evil of men can be forgiven if it all ultimately works out. Of course as a corollary, how toothless are good intentions when the results are evil? That seems the more unforgivable thing; faith is all fine and good but works are what put food in starving children's stomachs, antibiotics in sickly people's bodies, roofs over homeless heads. Maybe such pragmatism is the American in me asking "What's it worth?," or as is more likely the Catholic in me asking what good has been tangibly done, but I think that the old saw about faith being nothing without works is true. Judas was like all of us; a complicated mixture of good and bad where intent, action, and what's actually felt can be hard to disentangle. Noting that people are people and that some are evil and that some are good can muddle the issue of how goodness operates in the world. Goodness, rather, can be seen as a type of absolute force, an ever-reactive breath whose origins need not be from us but can prayerfully fill our lungs, forcing its way into the most crepuscular of spaces. A reading from the heretical bible which is only available to those living in Barbelo: "A good tree can sometimes bring forth evil fruit, and a corrupt tree can sometimes bring forth good fruit." Goodness is a rich soil, though sometimes very thinly spread upon the barren ground; and yet it's rich enough that even the sickliest of fallen mustard seeds can sometimes take sprout. Taking root in the driest of deserts. And though a reed makes not a full forest, it's still alive. Though it may not exonerate, redeem, or save the most malignant of souls, we need not be surprised when evil men can have their moment of grace, possessed by a tenderness they may not even be aware of, and pointing towards a sacred universe where we can never live but are sometimes made sacrosanct enough that we can gaze upon it.

XX

One evening Hakuin Ekaku encountered a samurai on the road. Resplendent in his red ochre armor, with immaculately carved wooden mask, the troubled samurai set out to find the great Rinzai monk, for the warrior feared that his sins would condemn him to hell. Hakuin had once felt fear at his own potential damnation, as frightened of hellfire as any of the contemporary mortifying Puritans who lived half-way around the world. After experiencing *satori* – on several different occasions I'll add – Hakuin developed the strict, if empathetic, rigors of Rinzai. For Hakuin reaching enlightenment wasn't enough; like revolution the fires of nirvana must be ever stoked. Among the commoners of eighteenth-century Japan, Hakuin was a bodhisattva who had conquered hell through *kaon*; who in true Zen fashion had time to do the dishes and laundry afterward (always remembering the most important things). So, this Tokugawa knight, perhaps straight from crucifying some Nagasaki Christians singing Japanese hymns translated by bearded Jesuit mandarins, searched for Hakuin to quiet his soul, to find peace and succor. And there, on that starless road (as I imagine it) in the shadow of Fuji, not far from his monastery Shōin-ji, the samurai first came upon Hakuin. "Great master," the warrior humbly asked, "tell me, is it true that there is a hell and heaven?" There was still in the night, the beginning of a slight autumnal chill here on the slopping green hill that reached up unto that great, sacred mountain. Crickets gently chirped. Water rushed over mossy, smooth black stones in a brook a few yards away. Hakuin remained silent, deliberating on the tortured samurai's question, before finally responding. "That is literally the dumbest fucking question I have ever heard." Without pause the samurai's disposition lifted. All of that tortured anguish replaced with incomparable rage. Who was this middling forest hermit to speak to him this way? And so the samurai unsheathed his sword and prepared to decapitate the monk. "Behold," Hakuin said, "the gates of hell." Satori. No longer intellectualized over, pined for, meditated on, reflected about, desired, described, or wished for, but achieved. His sword fell to the gingko blanketed floor of the path. "Behold," Hakuin said, "the gates of heaven."

XXI

The gates of hell. On June 23, 1691, the ironically named Mercy Brown, originally of the esteemed Tuttles, attacked her son Samuel with an axe in their Wallingford, Connecticut home. With one blow she cleaved the boy's head open like a rotten pumpkin hitting the stone floor, and would have decapitated him had her husband not wrestled the axe away. Though the family had been among the earliest settlers to New Haven, striking away from the backsliding they identified with Massachusetts, the Tuttles had long been associated with madness. Mercy's brother Benjamin was hanged for the very same crime she was guilty of, when he murdered their sister Sarah with an axe fifteen years before. The magistrates would be lenient with Mercy, rendering the judgment that, "she hath generally been in a crazed or distracted condition as well long before she committed the act, as at that time, and having observed since that she is in such a condition, do not see cause to pass sentence of death against her," electing rather to imprison her for life. Such mercy for Mercy may be due to the fact that for all of the violence of their crimes and their madness, the Tuttles were respectable Puritans. Mercy, for the heinousness of her act, had until that point been a decent, kind, and good woman. So solid were the Tuttles' religious bona fides that Mercy's grand-nephew was none other than Jonathan Edwards, the most brilliant of colonial American theologians. He who diagnosed humanity as being a "little, wretched, despicable creature; a worm, a mere nothing, and less than nothing; a vile insect that has risen up in contempt against the majesty of Heaven and earth" and so thus prescribed that we should "live in continual mortification, and never to expect or desire any worldly ease or pleasure." A clue as to what drove Mercy to her crime. Not Edwards of course (who wouldn't be born for more than another decade), but rather the theology of Calvinism. Five-point Calvinism (whose main principles of total depravity, unconditional election, limited atonement, irresistible grace, and perseverance of the saints are remembered through the charming mnemonic of TULIP) isn't anyone's idea of warm, with its emphasis on the total depravity of all humans, atonement limited to only an elect, and where grace is entirely unmerited by the sinful individual and only bestowed by God for inscrutable reasons. And most famously, the adherence to a strict belief in predestination. A Christian could never be certain of their salvation through any of their own actions, but there could be clues of one's status. Generally the elect were not murderers, fornicators, or sodomites. Members of the elect would have a clean conscious, which encouraged New England Puritans to examine their own minds with a psychoanalytically obsessive scrupulosity; tallying their thoughts, dreams, fears, and anxieties in exacting detail. Like Hakuin, who was six when Mercy Tuttle committed her crime an ocean and a continent away, she was obsessed with those flames of hell which eternally burn but give off no light. Calvinism is an exhausting way to live one's faith. Max Weber wrote about how the Calvinist was perennially engaged in discovering "the most suitable means of counteracting feelings of religious anxiety." For the Puritan, "the fundamental peculiarities of religious feeling" are defined by this uncertainty concerning their own election. Famously Weber argued that the capitalist accumulation of wealth and its reinvestment was spurred by such anxiety, as material success could be measured upon the celestial ledger of the individual soul as evidence of election. That would be at least one way to see if you were a member of the elect, but for many personalities it would be the uncertainty alone which would be horrific. One easy way to take the edge off would be to commit an act which would grant you certainty about the status of your election by confirming that you were not a member of the glorified. Such crimes were not unheard of, women and men so wracked by religious ambiguity that they were willing to commit atrocities for at least one bit of certainty, even if it was that they were bound for hell. It's the sort of crime that only the very genuinely and tortured pious can be capable of. Atheists may murder, but they don't do so to acquire knowledge of the state of their eternal soul. As James Hogg wrote in his 1824 Calvinist gothic masterpiece *The Private Memoirs and Confessions of a Justified Sinner,* "Nothing in the world delights a truly religious people so much, as consigning them to eternal damnation." So a frustrated, uncertain, and pious Mercy Tuttle who could not be assured of the Kingdom of Heaven rather conquered her anxiety by taking an axe and knocking open the very gates of hell. As her grand-nephew would preach, "You have reason to wonder that you are not already in hell."

XXII

The gates of heaven. What is more archetypally American than the serial killer? A boot-strapper, a rugged individualist, setting out west on the highway and rewriting the very rules of decency, of empathy, of morality, to suit their own twisted vision. A nihilistic cowboy roaming the plains of the depressing American backcountry dotted with strip malls and roadhouses, branding his innocent victims and dumping the bodies in shallow woodland creeks and trash-strewn alleyways. The highways of America crisscross the continent as deeply as the grooves of Charlie Starkweather's furrowed brow as he awaited his execution on Nebraska's death row. If the serial killer is prefigured by Jack the Ripper or Giles de Raise, then he now speaks with a twang. We're insatiable for their gruesome stories, craning our necks to gawk. All of those men with their middle names firmly repeated, lest we confuse them with some different, poor, innocent John Gacy. We read the detailed crime reports of Jeffrey Dahmer, Ted Bundy, the Zodiac Killer, and the Boston Strangler. Not satiated by stories of genuine evil, we invent them with our Hannibal Lecter and Buffalo Bill. The serial killer presents all of the rapacious, selfish, narcissistic greed of the American credo into its logical conclusion, which is why we're simultaneously attracted to and repelled. We talk about them as clinicians, they're "sociopaths" and "psychopaths," but that's just the gloss of medical language. We know what we really mean. As Hannibal Lecter himself said in Thomas Harris' 1988 *Silence of the Lambs*, "You can't reduce me to a set of influences. You've given up good and evil for behaviorism…You've got everybody in moral dignity pants – nothing is ever anybody's fault. Look at me, Officer Starling. Can you stand to say I'm evil?" In a disenchanted world, drained of meaning and significance, the serial killer offers us a depiction of transcendence by answering in the affirmative that evil is real. Not behaviorism, not criminology, but metaphysical evil. And where evil is proven to be real, we hope and pray that that implies good must be real as well. No modern writer more thoroughly explored the terrain of a quiet, faint, and whispered grace amid evil than did Flannery O'Connor. In the highway murder tale *A Good Man is Hard to Find*, she presents a disputation between a narcissistic old woman whose family has just been murdered and the man who did it, a serial killer known only as the Misfit. After marching her son, daughter-in-law, and grandchildren (including an infant) off to an execution, the Misfit returns to the grandmother. The two discuss Christ and his miracles, the Misfit (who claims to not even remember all of the murders he has committed, including that of his own father) expresses his doubts. For him, there is but one commandment, that there is "no pleasure but meanness." She reaches out to touch the Misfit's cheek, and says, "Why you're one of my babies. You're one of my own children!" Startled, he shoots the old woman three times in the head. While leaving the scene, one of his friends jokes about the "fun" which they just had, to which the Misfit replied there is "no real pleasure in life," concluding that the grandmother could have been a good woman if there "had been somebody there to shoot her every minute of her life." Critical debate has long centered on the change which seems to have occurred in both characters, even if the ultimate result of the interaction must still end in horrific violence. The Misfit has obviously been shaken by the tenderness afforded to him, a tenderness so out of character for the needling old woman we were previously confronted with. With her small world of small concerns, obsessed with social order and decorum, nostalgically pining for some lost agrarian Southern fantasy, she is a note-perfect portrayal of a hypocritical Christian. Yet her embrace of a man as evil as the Misfit is a consummate working of goodness through her, an impartation of grace from God onto her, and more importantly from her onto the killer. An act which if it does not save the killer certainly saves the grandmother. Joyce Carol Oates explores the similar demon haunted terrain of the serial killer in *The Girl with the Blackened Eye*. Her narrator recounts the horrifying details of her kidnapping, rape, and torture when she was only fifteen. She recollects how in his cabin the man "raped me, beat me, and shocked me with electrical cords and he stubbed cigarette butts on my stomach and breasts, and he said things to me." The serial killer in Oates' story is an irredeemable monster, like Lecter's imploration to Clarice Starling, it is impossible not to describe him as evil. And yet at the end of the story, with the girl chained up in his hidden cabin, the man uses his last bit of strength to draw a map for the police who've just critically wounded him, so that they can find and rescue the narrator. She writes, "He told them where the cabin was, when he was dying. He did that for me." Why did the man do this, why this mercy at the very end? Oates indicates that there could be psychosexual reasons, that he spared the girl once he realized she was younger than his favored targets. At one point, in between letting her eat greasy fried chicken and runny cole slaw as he picked ticks out of her matted hair in his weed filled backlot, he ruminates that, "There's some reason, I don't know yet, that you have been spared." Later on, sounding like the arbitrary God of the Calvinists, he tells her she would be saved because, *"You're not like the others. You're special. That's the reason."* His last seconds of strength were spent in ensuring that the girl would be saved. Was it enough to save his soul? Of course not. But it was enough to at least save her life. In his fictionalized song-version of the Starkweather murders, Bruce Springsteen sings "Well sir, I guess that there is just a meanness in this world." The promise and hope of grace is that no matter how small, or hard to identify, that perhaps there is a goodness in this world as well, even if it's not enough to save everybody, especially if sometimes there are brief seconds when even the most evil are capable of it.

XXIII

In the village of Faulksland, Germany, Johann Dunker would have just been another oddball if it wasn't for the very specific manner in which his eccentricity manifested itself. For example, there was Niles Schroeder, who would present to the tourists enjoying schnitzel and Riesling in the restaurants overlooking Lake Königssee neatly typed pamphlets he authored. Of varying degrees of word salad, the thrust of the meticulously thread-bound manifestoes was always the same – that for the crime of killing the Jews the German nation would be marked until the seventh generation. Because Schroeder had served with the fathers of the men who were the proprietors of these establishments, there was a tremendous degree of Teutonic latitude granted towards his tics. Schroeder had been a minor functionary at Dachau during the war, and though he had escaped the harshest of sentences, he was still detained by the Allies, and seems to have been affected a conversion at the hands of an American Baptist missionary. Faulksland had once been almost a third Jewish, but the Jews had been entirely murdered during the Holocaust in the early winter of 1940. Fully a quarter of the homes, now filled with German-speaking transplants from eastern Europe, had a small glimmering of fade next to their front doors where the mezuzahs had been pried off decades before. But for all of that haunting, no man made the citizens of Faulksland as uncomfortable as Dunker. He had moved there in 1947, a man of no history, no connections, no friends, and no memories. Dunker was observed acting in a rather odd manner for an ostensible gentile. From sundown on Friday to Saturday he refused to travel on the buses which were the pride of West German efficiency. It was noted that on those Sabbaths his house would go dark, no electric lights by which to illuminate. While shopping at the butcher shops which lined Max Plank Street at the center of Faulksland he never touched the Westphalian ham which was their pride. And after his death it was discovered that not only was his kitchen configured to maintain two sets of dishes, one for meat and one for milk, but that he had indeed utilized that arrangement for its express purpose, in a house that had once been occupied by a Jew long since immolated in the chimneys of Auschwitz. If the coroner who investigated Dunker's natural death some weeks after neighbors began to complain of the stench (though surely they must have smelled it before?) had suspected that the old man was a crypto-Jew, he was dissuaded by what he found next. For in an old carved wooden chest kept in a corner of his office, was his neatly pressed, immaculate, black, Waffen-SS uniform. And beneath the uniform, beneath his Iron Cross and the thankful accolades from Himmler and Hitler, below the black-and-white photos of a handsome young man, glass of schnapps in hand at Nazi Party functions smiling and raven-haired, were his diaries from 1940 until 1987 when he died, at the respectable age of 77. Do not be confused by these diaries, Dunker's narrative was not the same as that of Schroeder's. There was no contrition, no repentance. And there was no Johann Dunker, rather there was only Gerhart Schmidt, a mid-level Waffen official who had been responsible for the liquidation of Faulksland's Jews, some 12,960 men, women, and children. A treachery committed in distant Berlin with the filing of a few forms and the processing of some paperwork. A bit of bureaucratic malicious largesse for which, as the diaries indicate, he was exceedingly proud of, having chosen to make Faulksland his home. His anti-Semitism had not wavered in the years after his perverse "homecoming," if anything it had grown more virulent, evidencing an almost unimaginable sadism as he meditated on the deaths of the innocent Jews who had once lived in this town, had once lived in his home. Lest you think that Schmidt undertook his pantomime because of some distant Jewish ancestry, know that his Nordic lineage was substantiated by family trees that apparently went back to Charlemagne. For what reason did such a hateful man, a non-Jew, the murderer of Jews, so faithfully follow and adhere to Jewish law? His diaries make no mention of Levitical writ or Talmudic exegesis. But though the coroner discovered no testimony to why Schmidt should so faithfully execute the 613 commandments of God, he did find in a chest next to the Waffen-SS uniform a dingy cardboard box, inside of which were Sabbath candles, a worn *tallit*, a set of *tefillin* seemingly broken from overuse, and a frayed Hebrew prayer book, with the Kaddish underlined in red ink and the page consulted so many times that the ink of the Alephs, Bets, and Gimmels had been smudged to an ambiguous ashy gray smear. Why such a man as Gerhart Schmidt would uphold the law so completely has never been explained. If there can be understanding of a flame of some kind of perverse goodness in the soul of a man so malignant, it was advanced by the great Jewish philosopher and Holocaust survivor Adolph Trachtenberg, who in his 1989 *Newark Aphorisms* writes:

Schmidt then, was a strange instrument of God's justice. In this dark place where all the Jews had been eliminated, the Lord would at least ensure that the bright candle of Jewish practice could not be extinguished. And so to that end he forcibly compelled, as both punishment and as ineffable mitzvah, that the very agent responsible for that heinous crime would be he who fulfilled proper observance of the law, so that it should not perish from those environs, even if the people for whom it was originally commanded were dead, burnt upon the pyre by the very man now made to say Kiddush for them, the devil who consigned them to their nameless graves.

XXIV

I apologize for the macabre nature of my observations, but any discussion of good implies a consideration of evil. Writing this, as I am, with the world seemingly on the verge of nuclear war, what homily to goodness can be penned which doesn't sound cheap and disingenuous? Calvin once argued that all it would take to confirm God's benevolence would be the salvation of one man, one unworthy, degenerate, sickening worm of a man. Calvin's theology is a finely-wrought mechanical device, all of his pieces impeccable, every gear, and widget, and piston correctly fitted. Which is part of why it feels so cold, so empty. This then, has always been my difficulty with Calvinism, as expertly crafted as his syllogisms and postulates may be. If we are to cede that predestination is the ultimate expression of God's complete majestic sovereignty, if we are to affirm that individual agency implies a limitation in God's omnipotence, then why would you opt to believe in a form of double predestination whereby God condemns everyone to hellfire? Why should God be such a capricious creator? The salvation of one may be all that God requires to demonstrate His magnificence, but how much more so the salvation of two? Or of ten? Or 36? Or of everybody? If none of us has a choice in whether we receive grace, then how much more benevolent if we're all granted it? Debates over universal salvation would split the congregations composed of the descendants of New England Puritans like the Tuttles, as the rapacious intellectual energy of Calvinism turned itself inside out, with the limited atonement of Reformed theology transforming into an egalitarian atonement for all. Take Hosea Ballou, born of Huguenot extraction in rural New Hampshire four years before Concord and Lexington, son of a minister in that old non-conformist faith of the Baptists. His preaching, popular in the environs around Boston, split many Congregationalist churches such as the parish in West Cambridge, orthodox Calvinists,

Unitarians, and Universalists all electing to go their own way. The convulsions of late Puritanism, as it fractured and broke as completely as our Dead God from whom creation sprouts, were not weak tremors. Ballou converted to the Universalist faith the year of the French Revolution, and as the Jacobins stormed the Bastille, Ballou theologically stormed the gates of hell in hopes of abolishing that prison. With unfortunates such as the Tuttles in mind, Ballou wrote that Calvinism's preaching of "infernal torments...have tended so to harden the hearts of the professors of this religion, that they have exercised, toward their fellow creatures, a spirit of enmity." For Ballou, preaching in pulpits from Boston to Cambridge to Menotomy, the question of predestination had been incorrectly approached by the Calvinists. Yes, salvation requires God's freely given grace, but She does not limit Herself in its imparting, rather it is freely available to all. Furthermore, literally every soul would ultimately find redemption, no longer how long it takes. All of creation, no matter how low, filthy, debased, wicked, or malicious must ever reach upwards towards its Creator, yearning for a completeness whose experienced absence is the very hallmark of existence. Ballou, preaching in the first half of the nineteenth-century to an assembled congregation of Universalists in Menotomy's white steeple First Parish, topped with a celestial blue partial half-dome the color of the Virgin Mary's robe, sat both figuratively and literally half-way between the Unitarians just then putting their mark on Harvard Divinity School, and the tribe of Transcendentalists gathering in Concord. But Rev Ballou's doctrine was not original to him. The technical term for the final moment of universal salvation is *apocatastasis* – "reconstitution." Apocatastasis is a particular type of apocalypse, when all contradictions are reconciled, all inequities are leveled, all injustices are satiated, and *all souls are saved*. Apocatastasis marks the returning of all souls into a finality of eternal, infinite, universal goodness. In such a moment Mercy Tuttle is redeemed,

Hakuin's samurai is redeemed, the Misfit is redeemed, Gerhart Schmidt is redeemed, Judas is redeemed. In short, apocatastasis signifies the complete totalizing power of good. What then must any other experience of goodness be? They are reminders that though Utopia is no place, it can still be a republic of time. Utopia, and her sacred equivalent of Millennium, are not circumscribed by length, height, and width, but rather by duration. Utopia is not measured in distance, but in seconds. The experience of good is the impartation of a moment of grace, it offers us a window into the eternal realm of Millennium, a view of apocatastasis in the present. Goodness which reacts to evil, goodness which reacts to emptiness, goodness which reacts to loss, goodness which reacts to pain – such is the sacrosanct temple of the moment. Each moment of connection, of tenderness, of reflection, of intimacy, of truth, of beauty, of mercy, of empathy, of goodness is but a glimpse into that mystic domain of Millennium. Such moments are circumscribed, yet infinite: the omnipotent Republic of Grace. Ballou envisioned one grand moment whereby the Lord would embrace that great Adversary, and the task of creation would be complete, all redeemed in a shining flash of goodness. Do I imagine that will happen? I must confess, I have my doubts. And yet, such a moment of apocatastasis need not literally be true for us to have the deep intuitive knowledge that every moment of grace is still a reflection of that perfect, imaginary, illusory view of a world to come. Each experience of goodness, of grace, is a sacrament, prefiguring that ineffable potential of future completeness. Now, please consider: what if Judas did not kiss Christ to condemn Him, but rather that in that moment of grace Christ kissed Judas so as to bless him?

XXV

Who would have expected the origin to have been with a castration? A consummately violent act. Hacking away at flesh, and the discarding of that bit of intrinsic manhood. But Origen at that origin, in that moment, in that second, in that utopia, felt he had no other choice to unlock the door to the Kingdom of Heaven but by using the dull blade of a butcher's gelding knife on his balls. Sometime in the third century the Alexandrian monk, whose ruminations upon the Gospels were so often exquisitely beautiful, meandering digressions in the perfumed garden of allegory, read a crucial passage of Matthew and decided, with perilous results, to uncharacteristically interpret the Bible literally. Christ implores that "there be eunuchs, which have made themselves eunuchs for the kingdom of heaven's sake" and suddenly, at this most crucial juncture, a man for whom Genesis and Exodus were subtle allegory, decided that the Lord must have uttered this passage and meant it. Contradictions, contradictions, for Deuteronomy says that, "He that is wounded in the stones, or hath his privy member cut off, shall not enter into the congregation of the Lord," but for Origen it was apparently he who was without stones who would ironically be permitted to caste them. Origen, who embraced mystery and the apophatic had long preached that God himself must be ineffable that, "God is incomprehensible, and incapable of being measured," and it would seem that one day Origen decided that other things must cease to be capable of measurement as well. The Church Fathers, that collection of men who defined Christian theology in those crucial first centuries while gathered in sunbaked Egyptian monasteries, or upon tall pillars in the desert, or among the acidic shores of the Dead Sea, were a strange group. Jerome, tortured by his devils in the desert and consoled by his pet lion, or Simeon Stylites, the Stalactite who sat perched atop a huge column for 37 years outside of Aleppo, shitting down the sides and over the decades making his cylindrical platform look like nothing so much as a melting brown candle. But at least Simeon Stylites got to keep his nuts. Origen rather took that more exquisite path, the way of the castrator's blade, the better to separate himself from that tag of flesh which signified our connection to the birthright of our original sin. Origen's was a more radical circumcision, and as Abraham was promised that a great line would descend from him, Origen's severance of a few more inches would ensure that no such equivalent line would spring from his seed. I wonder what the psychology could be that would inspire one to take knife to scrotum, what fervency, what zealotry, and what greater ecstasy? Hard to imagine if we're being honest. But Origen, who made himself incomplete so as to be worthy of paradise, believed that that same paradise could only ever be achieved in that incompleteness. I wonder if, while that saw was pressed next to greasy flesh and fold of sack, he meditated upon that deity of his youth, who also crushed and shattered himself in hopes of a one day greater reward? When green-hued Osiris, god of the dead and Foremost of the Westerners, similarly stained Egyptian sands red with a sputter of blood from an organ more used to containing it? Osiris – king of the underworld and thus lord of the living – one of those perennially popular Mediterranean gods of resurrection. Mutilated by his brother Set, his organs and appendages scattered to every corner of the kingdom, evoking the harlot of Judges who was similarly mutilated. Devoted and loving Isis' task, in the various permutations of the myth, was to reassemble Osiris long enough so that he could impregnate her. But the irony was that of all the rediscovered limbs of the felled god, his penis alone remained hidden. And so the pantheon of other gods supplied Osiris with a golden phallus, and Isis was able to conceive their child Horus. Not for nothing in this tale of a resurrected member and god, but it was from the image of Isis holding Horus that the Egyptian Copts were first inspired to depict an infant deity in the arms of his loving mother and who would one day be similarly sacrificed. Whether cultural syncretism inspired Origen or not – for remember that the old gods still held firmly in Egyptian imaginations for half a millennia after the monk explicated the words of that other risen desert god – is impossible to know. But at the core of both stories is one of a whole being shattered into parts, and the possibility of reassembling those parts. They are about the nagging suspicion that something – something perhaps quite big – is missing. And the desire to return to wholeness, to order, to completion. Reading that bit of Matthew, which Origen so tragically misinterpreted, it's hard not to see that it couldn't possibly be asking the penitent to literally castrate themselves. Rather, in making oneself a eunuch for heaven, might Christ not have been claiming that we must sacrifice something huge, that we must make ourselves tender, vulnerable, wounded? And that paradoxically in this very shattering of self we come closer to the fullness of creation, for we have initiated the very process by which universal redemption must ultimately happen, by which slaying low we reach elevation, by becoming incomplete we approach fullness, that by being wounded we heal? And in that manner, I don't wonder if a regretful Origen had not a dream whereby he wandered through the dusty twilight streets of Alexandria, the sky a gloaming bloodish pink, and that like Isis among the Nile thrushes he found what he searched for. There, behind a rough tan pot full of olive oil, or a stall selling roasted dates, or on the winding stairs leading up to the lighthouse was his complete, disembodied, bloodless penis.

XXVI

Like so many who provided the intellectual scaffolding of early Christianity, Origen veered uncomfortably into heresy. Tertullian with his embrace of ecstatic Montanus and the latter's polyamorous apocalyptic Holy Spirit cult comes to mind. It's why we speak not of St Origen or St Tertullian. These were men for whom though they defined the very parameters of what makes orthodoxy such, departed enough from their very own definitions that they could never be honored with canonization. Too unseemly and torrid, thinkers who flitted about the forbidden margins of faith. Origen is one of these men, so central to the development of Christianity that he can't be exorcized, but not quite normative enough that we're going to have churches and Catholic schools named after him. Call it a variation on "The Tertullian Problem" – that the very man who coined the term "trinity" also ended up worshiping a con-artist who claimed to be a reincarnation of Jesus Christ while he traipsed through Asia Minor with his two prostitute wives. Origen's heresy was never quite as dramatic – the castration aside. And incidentally, it wasn't that occurrence which put him in slight disfavor in the Church, even if literalism is a rightfully recognized heresy in Catholic theology. Rather it was a different "inaccuracy" which condemned Origen the theological genius to the divine antechamber of purgatory, and that was the universalist theory of redemption embodied by the previously mentioned concept of *apocastasis*. For Origen, there was to be punishment but no eternal damnation. All iniquity would be reconciled, all sinners redeemed, all humans forgiven. And not just humans, for Origen hypothesized that Satan himself would be reconciled to God in the last moment of existence, and that a final act of contrition would bring creation to its conclusion. All the missing parts would finally be reconciled, as Isis had once discovered Osiris' member along the banks of the Nile – the ultimate goal would be completion, reconciliation, synthesis, unification. As an old teacher of mine used to quip, "Atonement might as well be at-one-ment." The sort of idea that, depending on one's inclinations, is either intensely attractive or a bunch of hippie bullshit. But universalism has had a venerable tradition, from Origen through to the liberal descendants of those New England Puritans, like the good Rev Ballou, who had once grown intoxicated on the sulfurous fumes of hellfire, but had since embraced more tolerant positions. Universalism is a variety of perennialism, an idea that whether it's correct or not is endlessly attractive to at least some people, and thus the Universalists of antebellum New England need not directly trace their lineage back to Origen, for their credo is one of those things that can emerge from time to time by virtue of its parsimony. Origen's contention that God "may recall all His creatures to one end, even His enemies being conquered and subdued." There is an innate attractiveness to finding these similarities in creed, that golden thread connecting Origen to Ballou. No doubt the latter must have been aware of the former, even if the historical cords connecting them are less direct than Ballou may have sometimes implied. One wishes to avoid that old fashioned, liberal Protestant reductionism which likes to see all of the world's religions as mere manifestations of a type of progressive Christianity, interpreting the Buddha as just another saint, or Muhammad as a social justice advocate. Religions are different from each other of course; if they weren't we'd be denying the wisdom that exists in traditions not our own. We'd refuse to see the beauty of the stranger, preferring to understand all encounters with the different into the narcissistic vanity of the mirror. And yet there is some truth that particular ideas reoccur with different vocabulary across denominations and faiths, whether the unity of God or the ecstatic unification of mysticism. Universalism – either by dint of it being a concept which is fundamentally attractive or by it actually being a true metaphysic – is represented in some form across all of the major religions of the world. More than a millennium after Origen put stylus to wax, and in the Old City of Jerusalem was born Isaac ben Solomon Luria Ashkenazi, who would come to be known by many of his followers as Ha'Ari: "The Lion." In the century of Luther, and Copernicus, and Elizabeth, and Shakespeare, the Ari lived in the dusty, backwater, desert homeland of his people. He settled in the town of Safed where he would gather disciples and teach. The Lion was steeped in the *Zohar*, and familiar with the sayings of mystical scholars like Rabbi Akiva and Shimon bar Yochai, men who had respectively journeyed into that primordial Garden and seen the Godhead unsheathed or who had contemplated the divine with every fiber of their being among the caves of the Levant. From their observations, Luria crafted his own response to the ruptures, injustices, and inequities of our clearly fallen world. In a city ruled by the Ottomans, filled with the exilic remnant of Jewish refugees expelled from Spain and Portugal, himself the child of the Ashkenazic victims of pogrom, the Ari was attuned to the ways in which our world was deeply and fundamentally broken. Yet his writing – recorded not in the arid syllogisms of theology but rather the ecstatic hymn of poetics – was a response and solution to our reality's fallenness. From his repose in the groves of pomegranate scented Safed, among the orange and lemon trees of warm Levantine springs, the Ari mounted his own kernel of resistance against the fallen kingdom of our material Earth. For Luria, all of us contained divine sparks, concealed in corrupted material husks, but there are ways in which we can rejoin those bits of energy to the fullness of the Godhead, a process which "releases the light from/the shells." In the variety of mystical Judaism which finds its inspiration in the writings of Ha'Ari, known as Lurianic kabbalah, there is discussion of that which existed before creation, of the *ein sof*, that is the infinite and ineffable ground of being which constituted that which we have imperfectly elected to call God. At creation the ein sof contracted with Itself to make room for the rest of the universe to expand out, a process called *zimzum*. God limited Itself, hollowed divinity out in what myth has called the "Fall," but which also allowed for an imperfect creation to exist. The goal of all existence since then has been *tikkun olam*, the healing of these cracks, fissures, and ruptures. It is in prayer, ecstasy, and most of all goodness that *tikkun olam* manifests itself, the restoration and elevation of those shards of divinity once cleaved off from the *ein sof*, all slowly to be restored towards that culminating revelation of what Origen would have recognized as *apocastasis*. For the Ari, the Sabbath was but a murky reflection of that coming universal harmony, of what Origen would call Millennium. A utopian space, carved out of the calendar of our corrupted years. One which gestures to that which could be done better, and the better which could be done perfectly. We are all fallen creatures, but in the theologies of both men, and innumerable others beside, it is in those moments of grace where we are afforded view of that which is elevated, elemental, eternal. Luria would have called such moments *mitzvoth*, Origen would have thought of them as good works, but what they are is remarkably similar. They are instances of the immaculate kindness that can act as a connection between human souls, the rare instances of goodness, compassion, and empathy that serve to mirror the possibility of a greater world that supposedly once was, and has yet to come (if it ever existed at all, if it ever can come at all). Origen wrote that "there are many christs in the world, who, like Him, have loved righteousness," and so coming very close to heresy Origen argued that we are all but little shards of light hidden within these material husks of our corrupted, temporary home; that there are many lamed vovniks. And if we are all christs, then it serves to reason that we can all have little versions of the love manifested at Calvary, little moments of atonement, little windows on paradise. There is a grand drama in the universalist promise of apocastasis, envisioning as it does that fallen Prince Lucifer embracing his Father in the last moments of ongoing creation and thus bringing an end to the whole process, but every act of loving kindness, of empathy, of forgiveness is but an example of that grand type. I am agnostic on final things, of if these windows of paradise look onto any actual reality at all. I am no utopian; no perfect republics shall be established on this Earth. And yet if the view is illusory, there is still great value in a window. For even if there is no universal reconciliation, it is a truth that all acts of kindness are but a kernel of resistance against the fallen world, that all are examples of that which can be better than what we so often are. Of this I cannot but help to affirm. There is – perhaps in our own time more than some – something radical in kindness, in tenderness, in vulnerability, in souls laid bare before each other. The very whiff of not just revolution, but more crucially of salvation. This then is the final axiom: that even if paradise is a country absent from all maps, that immaculate kindness remains the compass that can still orient us to paradise. That in the sublime moment of true human connection, of true kindness, there are intimations of heaven, even if no such place exists. That there is the face of God even if She is faceless, even if She doesn't exist at all. That kindness is, whether there be meaning or not, the only method and purpose to which we can ethically conduct ourselves. And that any account of goodness is but the contemplation of such moments, of gazing out through those windows onto fields of green shade where Isaac Luria sometimes composed his poetry, of knowing that there are no christs except each other. Of such goodness, of such sublime goodness, that we scarcely need be aware of anything such as angels, for we have perhaps glimpsed these things in the behavior of neighbors and strangers among us.

XXVII

The one and only time that Bill W. had a direct experience of God was December of 1934 at 293 Central Park West. Committed to a sanitarium because of his unquenchable thirst, for nothing had ameliorated the failed business man's dipsomania. He had spent stints in hospitals undergoing experimental treatments, signed pledges, made solemn and heartfelt promises to his long-suffering wife Lois, and though he could string together short periods of sober time, Bill W. couldn't help but return to his cups. Now, in the Charles B. Towns Hospital, treated with nightshade and shaking with delirium tremens, the middle-aged Vermonter, son of sober, stolid good New England Republicans, was at rock bottom. As he recounted, it was in the pit of blackest midnight despair that he cried out, "I'll do anything! Anything at all! If there be a God, let Him show Himself!" And then, as every great faith has its moment of theophany – Saul on the road to Damascus, young Muhammad hearing Gabriel, or Joseph Smith encountering Moroni – so too did Bill W. have a visitation from some sort of Higher Power. He remembers that "Suddenly, my room blazed with an indescribably white light. I was seized with an ecstasy beyond description...The light, the ecstasy – I was conscious of nothing else for a time...Then came the blazing thought, 'You are a free man.'" Bill W. thought to himself that this "must be the great reality. The God of the preachers." The great seventeenth-century French philosopher and mathematician Blaise Pascal had sewn into the lining of his coat a testament to his faith in the "God of Abraham, God of Isaac, God of Jacob, not of the philosophers and the scholars." Bill W.'s "God of the preachers" was a wholly more American God than Pascal's Old Testament deity, for the salesman's Lord was a God of his "own understanding." But a God that works is a God good enough, and indeed whatever Bill W. experienced off of Central Park West on that Depression era winter day did indeed seem to work. Perhaps a bit of the Ari's shards of light, or some trapped gnostic luminescence, whatever it had been it was something which utterly transformed the life of one of our most hopeless cases. But if you are assuming that this theophany, this mystical ecstasy, is an example of that kernel of resistance, the immaculate kindness that saves the world and which I wrote of in previous fragments, you are mistaken. Bill W.'s experience was perhaps some sort of abstract kindness that was imparted upon him, either from within or from without, perhaps the sort of grace that can save a soul, but ultimately not that which saves the world. No, for Bill W. that moment came a bit later, in May of the following year when he found himself in an Akron kitchen talking to a helpless physician whom history remembers as Dr Bob, and who in the spring of 1935 found that his morning hands would shake so much that he required a few shots of scotch so that he'd be able to perform his duties as a surgeon. Dr Bob was similarly as hopeless as Bill W. had once been, and had performed the requisite Stations of the Cross that made a show out of newly good behavior only to find himself saddled up at the same bars night after night. But now, talking with Bill, empathizing from him, drawing from his failures, his losses, his embarrassments, his shames, the two could rather instead find a common strength. In their conversations there was no "indescribably white light," no "ecstasy beyond description," just a group of drunks, but God all the same. Dr Bob recalled that rather than anything explicitly divine, what was of more importance in that initial meeting with Bill W. "was the fact that he was the first living human with whom I had ever talked, who knew what he was talking about...from actual experience. In other words, he talked my language." Let trumpets blare in scripture, and gods descend in myth, the only tangible goodness we have in this world is each other, and that realization, rather than just the intoxication of religious ecstasy, was Bill W.'s great genius. Lights and trumpets didn't keep Bill W. sober, nor did they keep Dr Bob on the wagon, but the communion of each other somehow did. If Americans have a particular brilliance for lived theology, then Bill W. is an underappreciated prophet, building a decentralized, non-hierarchical, wide-spread religion from bits of the Oxford Group, William James, Carl Jung, and the smithy of his own and others' lived experience, and whose churches are simply to be found at the front of the phone book. Writer Michael Tolkin explains that this religion which Bill W. and Dr Bob founded has:

> no dues, no tithes, no president, [is] protected from permanent officers and the development of cults by rotating leadership for each separate group, [has] no other requirement of membership than the declaration of fellowship in a shared condition…The making good on the American promise that all are welcome. This is not a new idea, but the first institution in America to make this idea real.

For Tolkin, this is "a religion that may yet save the world," but it is also a faith that offers not salvation precisely, and not redemption exactly, but the promise that no more did a person have to wake up with the shakes, or shitting blood, or in a pile of their own puke, delivered with a one-night respite from having almost choked to death. Or even more importantly knowing that they never again have to arise with The Fear. Trading in Eucharistic wine for instant coffee and cathedral sanctuaries for the bingo halls below, and yet such souls sitting in cheap folding chairs have been saved in those church cafeterias. Whatever else God can be defined as, Bill W. took that very American wisdom of the Transcendentalists and married it with a traveling salesman's intuition and brilliance for marketing to come up with a scripture speaking to particular needs at our very particular time, for as Tolkin explains, Bill W. understood that addiction is "the most modern affliction." It is "the terrible emotional complement to the assembly line in a consumer society" and that even if it is "a disease and not a sin" it still "demands moral responsibility for the cure of the disease." If there be disputation over the number and nature of the sacraments, Bill W. remains agnostic on the answer, save for the identification of one – human fellowship. Lights and trumpets are well and good, but it was with the kindness in telling Dr Bob that he understood his experience, and that things could be different, could be better, that Bill W.'s movement was started. With an act of kindness.

XXVIII

Alzheimer's is a disease which takes away, strips bare, and polishes the soul down to elemental nub. The life of the individual erases backwards, like one of those old recordable tapes slowly spooling to the first song, with God's thumb pressed down on the button of erasure. Pushing almost ninety, the poet Jack Gilbert spent his days sitting mostly catatonic in the assisted living facility overlooking foggy San Francisco Bay, where he ultimately died. Once the possessor of a nimble mind, Gilbert sang a song of the richness of interiority, the complexity of subjective experience, of a soul observing itself and the world. And now, because reality is cruel and ironic, the very depths of that mind filled in; Gilbert found his brain becoming a shallower and shallower body of water. The mystics speak of *kenosis*, of the hollowing out of self so that God can come in, but it would take a mean glibness to claim that there was any similarity between that process and what was happening to Gilbert. His collected works are as a spiritual biography of his experience, his mundane and yet totally profound collection of instances spent in a life almost a century long, but now that document was being deleted. The most recent memories would go first, the recent rediscovery by the national literary press upon the publication of his complete works, the feted profiles and the glowing reviews in *The New Yorker* and *The New York Times*, the interview in *The Paris Review*. Then beautiful Michiko, his wife whose love saved him so many times and who cancer took when she was only 36, and he already an old man. For whom Gilbert "came back from the funeral and crawled/around the apartment, crying hard,/searching for my wife's hair," trying to grasp with both tenderness and desperation the physical remnants of love lived honestly and intently, as one day he'd try to hold rapidly disappearing memories, as ephemeral as the thinness of a single long, black hair. Earlier lovers were subtracted; first Laura and then Linda, then Gianna. All of those places of quiet beauty that he had been fortunate enough to make his home over the decades similarly deleted, the "Paris afternoons on Buttes-Chaumont," the "Greek islands/with their fields of stone," the "beds with women, sometimes/amid their gentleness." A career recorded for posterity in the writing of literary critics but loosing from the grasp of Gilbert's own mind, volumes written whose contents were now inaccessible to his own recollection. *Tough Heaven* and *Refusing Heaven* and even *Views of Jeopardy* with that award from Yale when he was still a young man, forgotten by the very man who created them. Berkeley gone, Massachusetts gone, Japan gone, Greece gone, Denmark gone, England gone, New York gone. Finally even his beloved Pittsburgh, where he and his fellow poet Gerald Stern had once stumbled back from the Squirrel Cage on slippy snow-covered cobble-stoned streets in the dark depths of winter quoting Wordsworth, past stain-glass bejeweled brick row houses punctuating a sky "stained pink by the inferno always surging" in that city of "brick and tired wood." Those East Liberty alleys dusted white by the Lord Himself would disappear, as would the steel mills where Gilbert worked summers, noting that when surrounded by molten iron and Bessemer convertors pouring metal like it was golden glowing water it was impossible to "think small." Peabody High School would disappear, and that family home off of Penn Avenue, and finally Jack himself would vanish, gone, to wherever the milk of substance drains to when identity is gone. Or almost gone. When all else was forgotten, achievements and lovers, accolade and experience, what else could be left? In "remembering something maybe important that got lost?" The answer was always in his poetry, when he wrote that, "We find out the heart only by dismantling what/the heart knows." A friend visited him in the nursing home in the weeks before Gilbert died, now silent, now seemingly having forgotten everything, even the language which was once his medium and he its master. The friend held up a simple pencil and asked the poet if he knew what the word for it was. Gilbert couldn't place it, didn't remember. But he formulated an answer: "That's the thing that makes poetry."

XXIX

If, as Socrates argued, it's true that philosophy is simply preparation for death, then how much more so is poetry? For in verse there is the texture of life, from dewy morn to lonely night, from the drip of snow melting during a Pittsburgh spring to the scorching heat upon a fishing boat sailing the blue Mediterranean in the midst of a Greek summer. Physicians can explain the neurodegenerative specifics of the disease that marked Gilbert's last years, the entropy of neuron and the fraying of brain matter, but as with muscle memory the poet had written over the grooves of his soul with the specificity of lyric. In preparing for extinction, Gilbert created one of the most striking poems about the grandeur of life, regardless of whether meaning is objectively inherent or not. His *A Brief for the Defense* is morally sublime, for it boldly states how we should live every day even as the darkness grows, and implicit within it is the most pertinent of observations about the non-totalizing nature of goodness and the most important of commandments: to be kind. Gilbert, as for all of us, has no use for Panglossian bromides, for the cult of positive thinking, for unearned optimism. We must honestly admit that there is "Sorrow everywhere. Slaughter everywhere. If babies/are not starving someplace, they are starving/somewhere else." Optimism is prosaic, but hope is divine. Gilbert claims that "we enjoy our lives because that's what God wants," despite deprivation, despite death. No matter how horrific or how horrendous, how nihilistic or negating there "is laughter/every day in the terrible streets" for the "poor women/at the fountain are laughing together between/the suffering they have known and the awfulness/in their future, smiling and laughing while somebody/in the village is very sick." We laugh and enjoy and smile not in spite of the suffering implicit in all life, we laugh and enjoy and smile because of that suffering. We laugh and enjoy and smile not because we are inhuman, we laugh and enjoy and smile because we are human. And we love, "we enjoy our lives because that's what God wants." A crucial thought – the non-totalizing power of goodness is such that there is no hell where occasionally one can't feel joy, where one can't know love. There were prisoners in Auschwitz capable of sharing a joke with one another, there were survivors in Hiroshima who could observe the stars as beautiful. Gilbert's friend Stern remembered the end of the war, when in that "tiny living room/on Beachwood Boulevard" his family danced to *Bolero* in celebration, and danced in mourning for the millions of cousins turned to ash and smoke an ocean away. With "the world at last a meadow, / the three of us whirling and singing, the three of us/screaming and falling, as if we were dying." Gilbert knows that if "We deny our happiness, resist our satisfaction, /we lessen the importance of their deprivation." Such is the kernel of resistance, the ethic of kindness and delight, to "accept our gladness in the ruthless/ furnace of this world." Wisdom for "all the years of sorrow that are to come," whatever dystopia awaits, whatever nuclear conflagration, whatever oppressions, whatever strengthening of those old systems of injustice and whatever horrific novel inventions are approaching – that regardless "We must admit there will be music despite everything." Prepare yourself.

XXX

Margery Kempe was hard to like but easy to love; easy to love because in her insecurities, her fears, her sorrows, even her failings and most often her obnoxiousness she couldn't help but remind us of ourselves. Fourteenth and fifteenth-century England saw a veritable renaissance of vernacular sacred writing, from William Langland to the liturgical ruminations penned by Julian of Norwich. Kempe's contribution to this exemplary era was the first full autobiography to be written in the English tongue, a window into the ways that an individual consciousness can both torture and exult us, the mechanism of that soul's functioning in our fallen world. The devotional reasoning which knows that "wheresover God is, heaven is; and God is in your soul, and many an angel is round about your soul to guard it both night and day." All of what we know of her is from *The Book of Margery Kempe,* dictated by its illiterate author to two separate amanuenses, believed to first be her eldest son and then her priestly confessor. A remarkable book, quoted by Wynkyn de Worde in the early sixteenth-century, but in its entirety missing until its rediscovery in an attic in the 1930s. She was an unusually pious woman, even for an era half mis-remembered as being purely one of faith. Kempe's religious enthusiasms were extreme, not limited to just contemplation and prayer, or even pilgrimage, but indeed for the copious tears which stand out to any reader of *The Book of Margery Kempe* as one of the most extreme aspects of the autobiography. Kempe cries in sorrow, in adoration, in ecstasy. Author Colin Dickey, reflecting on this saintly woman who was a bit too human to ever actually be recognized as a saint, writes that, "More than laughter, mourning, or sex, crying (which can encompass all of these things) is the truly excessive gesture, the limit of emotion available to us." If anything in our profane existences can qualify as *kenosis,* it might as well be our tears, and if that be the case then Kempe was one of the holiest empties who ever prayed on this Earth. Dickey observes that you "cannot open her autobiography anywhere without stumbling on a passage of her weeping; it saturates the text." Kempe, who dictated the book in the third person and who when she didn't refer to herself by her own name called herself "creature" (as in one who was created by God) recorded that "Her weeping was so plentiful and so continual that many people thought that she could weep and leave off when she wanted, and therefore many peoples said she was a false hypocrite, and wept when in company for advantage and profit." As a result of her often strange behavior she faced accusations of heresy at several points, though she was acquitted of any of those accusations of Lollardy as they emerged. But that's not to speak of more personal tribulations, any one of which deserve tears, albeit perhaps not ones of as extreme a frequency as those of the author's. Kempe, mother of fourteen children who seemingly always wished more to be an anchoress rather than the self-made brewer that she was, who suffered a profound post-partum depression after the birth of her eldest which led to delusions of being tortured by demons, who had to nurse her husband through a debilitating illness and watch him die, and who was threatened with rape when arrested on those previously mentioned heresy charges. Scholars of later periods of literary history can tend to regard the medieval as uncanny, as strangely inhuman. We sometimes argue that this is a period where the writers lacked "interiority," where individuality was defuse and undifferentiated. But whatever seeming lack of subjectivity exists in the period, Kempe's memoir disavows us that it was because the people were substantially foreign in comparison to us. Part of what makes her account so moving is that it isn't a hagiography, that her failings and desires are so on display to us. What has always affected me the most about *The Book of Margery Kempe* isn't her saintliness, but how often she falls short, in her simultaneous doubts and misplaced scrupulosity. What moves me is the book's exquisite sadness. In particular, her relationship with her husband (for unlike so many saints, Kempe was no virgin, something which grieved her). She writes that "this creature advised her husband to live chaste and said that they had often (she well knew) displeased God by their inordinate love, and the great delight that each of them had in using the other's bodies." What first struck me when I encountered that passage was the blunt confession of sexual desire for her husband; these two *loved one another*. And then what should strike the reader is how profoundly sad it is that her piety caused her guilt over that love. The two had what was known as a "chaste marriage" (at least after their fourteen children), an arrangement which the two of them struggled with. In another passage, Kempe writes how:

> this creature was coming from York carrying a bottle of beer in her hand, and her husband a cake tucked inside his clothes against his chest – that her husband asked his wife this question: 'Margery, if there came a man with a sword who would strike off my head unless I made love with you as I used to do before, tell me on your conscience – for you say you will not lie – whether you would allow my head to be cut off or else allow me to make love with you again, as I did at one time?'

In my dog-eared and underlined copy of *The Book of Margery Kempe* I scrawled a bit of red marginalia: "something about this line of questioning is so sad," an assessment that a decade after having first read her book I still assent to. Lest one think that it was only her husband who had misgivings about their new celibacy, turn to the passage in which she admits that "if she saw a handsome man, she had great pain to look at him, lest she see him who was both God and man. And therefore she cried many times and often when she met a handsome man," simultaneously attracted to the idea of Christ's physicality and repulsed at her own attraction to sensuousness more generally – and fully admitting to looking at men other than her husband. What Kempe, finally, offers us is not her tears or her prayers, but the perspective of just another flawed subjectivity such as our own, another soul trying to do good but so often falling into frustration and myopia and the hubris of faith. Writing of her husband, she explains how she:

> had very much trouble with him, for in his last days he turned childish and lacked reason, so that he could not go to a stool to relive himself, or else he would not, but like a child discharged his excrement into his linen clothes as he sat there by the fire or at the table... many times she would have disliked her work, except that she thought to herself how she in her young days had had very many delectable thoughts, physical lust, and inordinate love for his body. And therefore she was glad to be punished by means of the same body.

She may have wished to be a saint – all saints perhaps wish to be saints – but she was not one. As perhaps there are no saints. Rather Kempe was simply a person, one who could love and grow frustrated with those whom she loved, as all people do. And in an era where hagiographies were recorded in stain glass and vellum, *The Book of Margery Kempe* records the activities of a totally more fatiguing, annoying, frustrating, and thus human person, and it is all the more sacred for it. What Kempe offers is occasional empathy and sometimes meanness, as we all do, for who does not find themselves occasionally tender and sometimes short? Dickey explains that "Margery Kempe, finally exhausted by tears, turned to words and traded the immortal life of a saint for the immortal life of a writer." Her immaculate moment of kindness which she offered was her writing, for from the fifteenth-century until today Margery has given us a view into her mind, into her soul, and what we see is somebody who in all of her imperfections is like nobody so much as ourselves. Somebody always trying to be better and so often falling short, sometimes falling short precisely because of the things she does to try and be better. No superior mechanism for empathy has been developed than writing, no engine for sympathy more finely wrought than literature. Kempe's kindness is finally not even necessarily that which she showed in the book – in tending to her ill husband or praying for her children – rather it's in giving us the ability to show her kindness, to show her empathy, in being able to read her book and to feel that warmth of recognition, that comfort of familiarity. Kempe's kindness, the honest writer's kindness, is letting us know her and giving us the opportunity in felt connection (even if she be dead) to feel kindness back at her. Pray for souls in purgatory, but better to read the words written by those occupants. To be able to read such a sad pronouncement of that almost-saint that "She thought that she loved God more than he loved her," and to wish that you were able to embrace her and tell her that it doesn't matter, since we love her. And to whisper to her that ever true observation of her contemporary and confidant Dame Julian of Norwich, who reminds us that "all shall be well; and all shall be well; and all manner of things shall be well."

XXXI

If Margery Kempe's salvation was in writing, then the character of Vivian Bearing in Margaret Edson's sublime play *W;t* experiences a type of salvation through reading, first by a squandered opportunity and then later through the gift of a selfless love. A scholar of seventeenth-century metaphysical poetry, more specifically the *Holy Sonnets* of John Donne, the play begins with Vivian's diagnosis of stage IV ovarian cancer, and follows through with her reflections on her scholarship, her role as a subject in a new experimental treatment, and finally her death. Edson is a nurse by training, and *W;t* conveys one of the most basic observations of any ethic – that our kindness and morality must always stem from the awareness that we are embodied creatures, with all the frailty and indignity which that implies. Cancer, that "emperor of maladies" as physician Siddhartha Mukherjee calls it, has rarely been represented in popular culture or art with the full impact of its awful power. Reduced to colored ribbons and glib t-shirt phrases which imply that all we need do is "race" and a cure shall be found. Seemingly omnipresent and completely absent, "cancer" is quietly uttered as if a curse, and the perennially cheery American ethos is such that the disease can be presented as a means for self-growth and discovery. Cancer patients, when depicted on television or in film, are at most shown wearing that red bandana of courage and otherwise looking like the hale and healthy California actors who no doubt portray them. They are rarely presented as emaciated, as covered in sores, as in continual pain, as cadaverous, though cancer patients often exactly look like that and feel like that. Cancer is a negation of the body, a subtraction that is paradoxically accomplished through a cellular addition: the perverse irony of your own physical being turning against you. There are no lessons in cancer. It is not a morality tale, or a war, or something for which there are survivors and losers.

Cancer is the betrayal of the body, painful in a meaningless way, and then often it kills you. Edson and her play never forget that simple fact, and that's why it's one of the most crucial depictions of the disease: because the play understands. There is no shying away from the depiction of what stage IV metastatic ovarian cancer does, as Vivian reminds the audience to whom she continually addresses herself. "There is no stage five." Edson presents cancer as not simply a disease which gives the patient a bit of a haircut, but rather, as her oncologist Dr Kelekian rather clinically describes it, a disease where the "antineoplastic [treatment] will inevitably affect some healthy cells, including those lining the gastrointestinal tract from the lips to the anus," in which the professor is made to endure "eight treatments of Hexamethophophacil and Vinplatin at the *full* dose." Early on Vivian tells the audience that the cancer treatment "is highly educational. I am learning to suffer," and indeed if there is any line which fully conveys the singularity of her experience in a play that is ironically filled with finely-wrought lines, and is in part about the beauty and failure of finely-wrought lines, it's the almost absurdly prosaic "Oh, God, it is so painful. So painful. So much pain. So much pain" which is delivered with scalp shrinking horror by Emma Thompson in the film adaptation. Dr Bearing, a scholar whose entire professional reputation is built on her ingenious interpretations of some of the most exquisite language ever crafted, suddenly finds that language completely fails her when she is confronted with the inexplicable enormity of pain. Literary critic Elaine Scarry, our great theorist of pain, writes that "Whatever pain achieves, it achieves in part through its unsharability, and it ensures this unsharability through its resistance to language...Physical pain does not simply resist language but actively destroys it." This is deeply and importantly true, and it is in part what *W;t* is about. Sometimes the play is remembered as being purely concerned with medical detachment as exemplified by the clinical coldness of Dr Kelekian and his arrogant resident Jason. And in part *W;t* is about that, but more accurately the play takes as its subject the failure of all language. Not just the technical jargon of the doctor and of inexact metaphor, but the failure of poetic language as well. Any humanist who watches *W;t* and sees only excoriation of science is a humanist lacking in introspection, for Kelekian and Jason's failures of epistemology are mirrored by Vivian herself. Early on, with no less hubris than Jason, she tells us that she knows "all about life and death. I am, after all, a scholar of Donne's Holy Sonnets, which explore mortality in greater depth than any other body of work in the English language." Edson makes the parallels between Vivian and Jason (who was a former undergraduate of hers) clear: as Jason can't help but see cancer in purely clinical terms, Vivian similarly can only understand the poetry which she studies as constituting objects which exist to demonstrate her brilliance (which they do). She describes metaphysical poetry as "a way to see how good you really are." But as she sees no disjunction with using the corpus of Donne's melancholic art as a means of professionally moving up through academe (with the added pleasure of intellectually shaming lesser scholars) she fears a similar lack of empathy in Jason, describing the inevitable journal article that Kelekian and he will write as not being "about *me*," but rather "about my ovaries. It will be about my peritoneal cavity, which, despite their best intentions, is now crawling with cancer. What we have come to think of as me is, in fact, just the specimen jar, just the dust jacket, just the white piece of paper that bears the little black marks." What a revealing metaphor – Jason will treat Dr Bearing's body as simply a book, a "white piece of paper that bears the little black marks." Of course that is exactly how she has so successfully approached the poetry of Donne. In flashback we are treated to Vivian in her intellectual prime, in discussion with her graduate committee chair E.M. Ashford, as a young teacher taking a bit of sadistic thrill in demonstrating to her students the depths of their ignorance, in asides in which she mocks the intelligence of her humane nurse, Susie. She informs us that she was a graduate assistant on her adviser's edition of *Devotions Upon Emergent Occasions,* appropriately enough Donne's profound meditation upon his own convalescence, and yet all of this sheer and undeniable intellect abandons her the moment she faces not just her own demise, but *pain.* Towards the end of *W;t* she says to the audience that, "We are discussing life and death, and not in the abstract, either; we are discussing *my* life and *my* death, and my brain is dulling." The play may be about the failure of science (not for nothing is it sometimes taught in palliative care courses), but just as crucially it is about the failure of art. Or at least about a certain approach to art, of Vivian's attitude towards literature. A different approach is suggested by the example of Ashford, her former professor. In a flashback we're privy to a conference between the two, when young Vivian has written a close reading of Donne's *Holy Sonnet X* based on the so-called "Revised Sequence" of 1635, which departed from the original manuscripts by "correcting" the poet's idiosyncratic punctuation and forcing it into something more conventional for the time period. Ashford excoriates Vivian for not going to the Westmoreland sequence which was closer to Donne's intent. The edition used by Vivian traded in the subtleties of Donne's original punctuation for the definitive drama of exclamation marks, semicolons, and capitalization. But as Ashford explains to her student, the sonnet is:

> ultimately above overcoming the seemingly insuperable barriers separating life, death, and eternal life...Nothing but a breath – a comma – separates life from life everlasting. It is very simple really. With the proximal punctuation restored, death is no longer something to act out on stage, with exclamation points. It's a comma, a pause. This way, the uncompromising way, one learns something from this poem,

wouldn't you say? Life, death. Soul, God. Past, present. Not insuperable barriers, not semicolons, just a comma.

But for all of her skills of critical analysis, Vivian is lost when it comes to her professor's close reading: "The insuperable barrier between one thing and another is... just a comma? Simple human truth, uncompromising scholarly standards? They're *connected?* I just couldn't..." Donne's final line, "And death shall be no more, Death, thou shalt die," is not postulate, it is not contention, it is certainly not *wisdom,* for Vivian Bearing it is simply the experimental field on which she can demonstrate her own acute and unforgiving intelligence. But reading is nothing if not an act of faith. Analysis, close reading, *explicacion du texte,* all have their place as assistant to that honest and inquiring faith, but ultimately it is the clear heart assisted by the head which makes a poem purposeful, not that head by itself. Vivian can interpret the poem, but what it means remains beyond her abilities. Which makes the penultimate scene of the play all the more moving, because Dr Ashford visits Vivian on the eve of the former student's death, the only visitor during the entirety of her illness. At this point Vivian's cancer has progressed beyond any repair, and her pain is so consuming that she has ceased to be verbal beyond monosyllables. Dr Ashford, who has had a career every bit as illustrious as Vivian's, is in the unnamed city to visit her great-grandson on the occasion of his fifth birthday, and only discovered her most promising pupil's illness upon stopping by the English department and learning of Vivian's treatment at the university medical center. In a play about a humanist, the most potent scene of humanity is this one. Ashford asks Vivian if she wants something recited, "Would you like that? I'll recite something by Donne." Vivian's only response is a gasped "No," and so Ashford rather elects to read to her student something a bit more elementary, a present she has brought for her great-grandson: *The Runaway Bunny* by Margaret Wise

Brown. The graduate adviser, cradling her now skeletal former charge as if she was her own daughter, reads the children's book to the dying woman. Two brilliant scholars, experts on the most difficult poetry written in our language, sharing in that communion of language, and the text under consideration is *The Runaway Bunny*. And the humanity of Edson's play is that they're not the less for it, far from it. Ashford dutifully recites all of the permutations that the titular bunny takes in Wilson's picture book, from trout to bird and so on, eventually uttering the pedagogical aside "Look at that. A little allegory of the soul. No matter where it hides, God will find it. See, Vivian." What Edson depicts is a sort of teacherly salvation, a type of redemption through reading. Vivian is not a bad person, she never was, but she was very much a broken person. In setting up the contrast between Ashford and Bearing, Edson's play shows us two different models of instruction, two different models of reading. Vivian's career was built entirely upon demonstrating her acute intelligence, but her dissertation chair's perspective has been that "one learns something from" either Donne, or *The Runaway Bunny*. This moment – inescapably beautiful, quiet, and sad – with the adviser cradling her dying pupil, is one of the most painfully intimate in contemporary American drama. The moment of kindness for Vivian and for the audience is when Ashford tells her student that "It's time to go. And flights of angels sing thee to thy rest." We believe it not just because it's beautiful, but because maybe it's true.

XXXII

So many figures to blame for modernity – Luther, Darwin, Freud. But as the solstice of our era approaches, that coming midnight of the century with the occluded clouds of Dionysius once again rolling West, and Frederic Nietzsche seems increasingly responsible for whatever death of truth we now face. Nietzsche, with his drooping walrus mustache and those sad Teutonic eyes, always an ever-attractive figure for other sad young men who parrot lines from *Thus Spake Zarathustra* or *The Antichrist*. Blamed, rightly or wrongly, for both fascism and anarchism (though I'll admit that if he's the progenitor of the latter my estimation of his politics would rise quite a bit), he's one of those ambivalent figures in intellectual history, rightly prized for his prose style as much as for the content of his thoughts. Mythic, cryptic, gnomic, aphoristic – Nietzsche could turn a phrase that had the quality of scripture, ironically utilized for the most antinomian of purposes. For whom there "are no facts, only interpretations" and "no philosopher is more correct than the cynic." The proverbs of hell: "Life is not a product of morality," "everyone feels superior to everyone else," "To see others suffer does one good, to make others suffer even more," "That every will must consider every other will its equal — would be a principle hostile to life, an agent of the dissolution and destruction of man, an attempt to assassinate the future of man, a sign of weariness, a secret path to nothingness," "The sick are the greatest danger for the healthy; it is not from the strongest that harm comes to the strong, but from the weakest," "Whom do I hate most among the rabble of today? The socialist rabble... The source of wrong is never unequal rights but the claim of 'equal' rights," "We do not believe in any right that is not supported by the power of enforcement," and of course "God is dead." Readers of much greater erudition than I can formulate arguments as to how Nietzsche utilized poetics, metaphor, allegory, fabulism, and fable to construct

91

complex modern myths. Where simply ascribing any particular, literal belief to the philosopher risks falling into simple-minded fallaciousness. That's fine – I still suspect that he was probably a pretty unpleasant man to know. Even if claims that he's responsible for Nazism or totalitarianism are overblown, and especially if his claim that he was "no man" but rather that "I am dynamite" are similarly grandiose, it's undeniable that he cuts a wide swatch on the intellectual history of the last century. Placing him in a correct lineage of ideas may be difficult, but it's obvious that there are certain values he seemed to uphold over others – the ethic of strong over weak, powerful over powerless, pleasure over morality, the individual over community, other humans, or God (only so much bourgeoisie affectations). One would imagine that he might feel that 36 observations about goodness are 36 too many. Was Nietzsche a cold man, a hard man, a cruel man? Was he a mean man, an angry man, a tough man? Was he the anti-Christ he seemed to proclaim himself to be? I know nothing about any of that, leave it to the academic philosophers to suss that out. What I do know is that however cold he may have been, however hard, cruel, mean, angry, tough, or anti-Christian, however much he celebrated strength, power, pleasure, and himself over the values of us democratic sheep, that if there is any redemptive moment in simple human kindness, Nietzsche ironically exemplifies it. For, as according to the popular legend, the last free moment the philosopher had in public before he succumbed to syphilitic psychosis was on January 3, 1889, when walking on the Piazza Carlo Alberto in Turin, he came upon a poor horse being violently flogged by its owner, ran up to embrace the weak, defenseless creature so as to save it, and collapsed never to utter another sane thought again.

XXXIII

Vladimir Nabokov, that old White Russian and master of two tongues, wrote in his memoir that "The cradle rocks above an abyss, and common sense tells us that our existence is but a brief crack of light between two eternities of darkness." The depth of my inexperience is too profound for me to ever quite have the confidence he has that an eternity of darkness exists on either side of that brief crack of light which constitutes my life. I've heard the observation ascribed to Lucretius (or is it Democritus?) that fear of the finality of death is foolish, for we are not apprehensive about the non-existence which preceded our birth. To which I say, any person not fearful of having had no face before their first birthday is a person who is not living their fear creatively enough. But immortality is not what I've come to write about, rather I wish to repurpose Nabokov's observation by way of a *quad erat demonstrandum*. That is that whether or not there shall be an eternity of darkness stretching before our birth or after our death, it seems unequivocal that a moral eternal darkness certainly permeates our living moments, perhaps in our own age as much as any. Let the moral utilitarians foolishly argue that violence has been reduced, or that we're headed towards a positivist utopia based on technocratic pragmatism. The gut knows what the algorithm doesn't. For in an era in which several countries have the technological ability to destroy the world dozens of times over by reducing it to cold radioactive ash, what counter argument need be formulated against cheery optimism? What calculus of pluck can be commandeered to claim that a veritable golden age of digital freedom stretches ahead, that people are somehow more fundamentally decent now than in the past? For in a period that bottles such horrific violence in the concentrated vial of potentiality that defines the nuclear predicament, one can't credibly claim that ours is a good age. The abyss that the cradle rocks above is not death, it is our life now, and the eternity of darkness stretches not before and after, but rather throughout. And yet there is that crack of light, still there, and however faint as the night grows blacker, it can provide all of the more striking a glow so that you can read the face of those next to you.

XXXIV

One summer, after watching my father die from cancer and finding myself too often hungover, I decided to write an essay about John Donne and Hiroshima:

A dark vision – it is the midnight of our age, and the world's last night. New York, Washington, Moscow, Beijing, Berlin, London, all the great cities of the world destroyed in whatever war is to come. St Paul's Cathedral once laid waste in the Great Fire of the late seventeenth century and almost destroyed again in the blitz of 1940 finds itself in ruins. In the debris one can make out the remains of a chapel built in honor of the men that perished in that last world war. It is dedicated to the Americans who fought alongside the British, and facing that chapel is a statue of John Donne, the base of which is still black from the flames that almost destroyed London in 1666. In this way Donne stares at an America to which he always wished to journey and to which he never did. The statue is based on a drawing of Donne in his death shroud, made while he was still alive, and which he hoped would depict how he would look upon his resurrection at the Day of Judgment. Now I ask, J. Robert Oppenheimer may have convinced us of the reality of apocalypse, but how many of us are naïve enough to still believe in Donne's millennium which would follow? Can Donne's grave be broken up again, can any of ours, can the world's? After such death who can still believe in resurrection? Who among us has faith that on that last day the dead eyes of Donne's funeral statue will be able to finally open, and that if he could, he would be able to see anything left in that west? Can we still believe in spite of it all? Evidence of hope: after the destruction of Hiroshima the official United States military report predicted that the soil in the city would be so radioactive that nothing would be

95

able to grow there until the year 2020. Yet in the autumn of 1945 a photographer took a photo of a single red canna flower growing through the rubble of the destroyed city. Donne writes: 'And Death shall be no more, Death, thou shalt die.'

Of commas and flowers and single lights we pray.

XXXV

On the day that the towers fell, Fr Mychal Judge's dead body
was cradled by the rough men of the FDNY who had constituted
his flock. Carried out of the lobby of the north tower shortly
before it would collapse, photographs of the gentle Franciscan
priest depict nothing so much as a *pieta*, Mary's white hands
replaced by the calloused and dirty paws of the fire-fighters
for whom this man acted as chaplain. In the late afternoon of
that sunny day of immaculate cloudless blue skies Fr Mychal
had rushed to lower Manhattan to administer the sacrament
of extreme unction to those dying in what remained of the
burning candle of the World Trade Center. A total of 107 floors
below the smoking rubble above, and Fr Mychal consoled the
dying, dutifully and faithfully repeating liturgical promises,
his Brooklyn accent slightly rounded out by the brogue of his
parents' County Leitrim. He was struck dead by a bit of debris
while giving someone else their last rites. On a day that would
take almost 3,000 lives, and how ever incalculable more of those
survivors extinguished from the deaths of their loved ones, from
suicide, addiction, or black lungs diseased from the pulverized
remnants of life which became the atmosphere of New York
that day and the day after, Fr Mychal would forever be listed
as "Victim 0001." That day of infamy when everything started
to go wrong, this day of sorrow, when in the fiery wreckage
there were so many moments of human kindness, of human
connection, those strangers who rather than asphyxiate would
clasp hands together as if they had known each other their whole
lives while taking that leap of faith into oblivion rather than
burning to death. Men and women who led people whose names
they didn't know to safety through pockmarked stairwells. All
those who perished in what the poet Martin Espada described
as the "thunder wilder than thunder." Would you give your life
to someone whose name you didn't know, whose face you never

saw? I'm not sure that I would, but many have, and do, and will, and that is enough to demonstrate goodness. Fr Mychal was one who did, even as the literal world collapsed around him, as Babel fell. But this is not the moment of immaculate human kindness, of selfless mercy, which I have in mind for this observation. For Fr Mychal knew those streets of lower Manhattan well, and before he was Victim 0001 he recognized Christ in the face of the homeless, the junkie, and most of all the victim of that plague which once ravaged this city so completely. Fr Mychal was a gay man, who saw no disjuncture between that identity and following the dictates of St Francis. He acknowledged being a gay man, a faithful Catholic, a devoted priest always trying to fulfill his obligation. He was no hypocrite – he saddled himself with the hair-shirt of celibacy, faithfully holding to the inhuman decrees of his beloved Church, denying himself the love that is every human's consolation, but while also refusing to see himself as deviant, broken, wrong. Most crucially his was the love, the *agape,* of the priest who refused to see others who were like him as being deviant, broken, or wrong. As he said, "Is there so much love in the world that we can afford to discriminate against any kind of love?" Decades before his death, when thousands of men had died in lower Manhattan streets, thousands more than would ever die on that one day in the new millennium, and Fr Mychal had already lived the liturgy of the living God. In the 1980s, when so many young men came from every corner of this empire to Chelsea, and the East Village, and Tribeca, and the Village to live lives free and full of love only to be struck down by what they called the "gay cancer" – Fr Mychal would console them. When many were abandoned to death by their families – Fr Mychal would hold them. When many feared contracting the disease and hospitals were so filled with the convulsions of beautiful, dying young men – Fr Mychal would sing to them; Fr Mychal would pray to them. When Ed Koch felt contented by comforts of the closet, and Ronald Reagan's press secretary could mock the queers dying from this disease, and when the Archdiocese could continue to pretend to be blind and many of the faithful could pretend deep in their black hearts that such suffering was part of any god's plan, Fr Mychal was on Canal and MacDougal and Clinton and Bowery with the junkies and the hustlers and the gays. With God's people. On that hot September day, Fr Mychal was ready, for he'd already been used to administering the sacraments while the world collapsed around him. It's not his fault if most people hadn't been willing to notice those collapsing worlds before, for a monument to the thousands who died in those early days of that epidemic was only finally erected in 2016. The priest visited one of those men on the day that that man died. A once strong man, now barely 80 pounds; once young, now with an aged, crippled body; once beautiful, now a living cadaver. The man – perhaps from a religious family who had abandoned him, perhaps very far from his home – with labored, sallow breathes posed to Fr Mychal one of the saddest questions that can be asked: "Does God hate me?" And St Mychal heard his prayer, and St Mychal answered him, and so St Mychal held him in his arms and gently kissed his forehead on the night that he died. I think that he was a very good man.

XXXVI

So. To whatever being there is, to the sacred, to the holy, to the nothing, to each other; who are in heaven, Earth, and everywhere in between; hallowed be your names, all of them; for though the kingdom may never come there are still those moments of grace, kindness, and love; and for that all of our will must be done; especially on Earth, for who knows if there is a heaven? Give us our bread, and our roses too, give us our moments, and mercies, and kindnesses as well; and please forgive us our trespasses, failures, flaws, frailties, brokenness, and humanity; as we attempt and too often fail to forgive those who trespass against us, and as we attempt to reach out and embrace those whom we should embrace lest we not be embraced in return; and lead us not into temptation; but deliver us with that piercing light which illuminates the ever encroaching darkness, so that we may be better able to see each other and to fulfill that one indispensable commandment – to be kind so that we may be good. And all shall be alright, and everything will be ok, and all manner of things shall be well. Amen.

CULTURE, SOCIETY & POLITICS

Contemporary culture has eliminated the concept and public
figure of the intellectual. A cretinous anti-intellectualism
presides, cheer-led by hacks in the pay of multinational
corporations who reassure their bored readers that there is no
need to rouse themselves from their stupor. Zer0 Books knows
that another kind of discourse – intellectual without being
academic, popular without being populist – is not only possible:
it is already flourishing. Zer0 is convinced that in the unthinking,
blandly consensual culture in which we live, critical and engaged
theoretical reflection is more important than ever before.
If you have enjoyed this book, why not tell other readers by
posting a review on your preferred book site.

Recent bestsellers from Zero Books are:

In the Dust of This Planet
Horror of Philosophy vol. 1
Eugene Thacker
In the first of a series of three books on the Horror of Philosophy,
In the Dust of This Planet offers the genre of horror as a way of
thinking about the unthinkable.
Paperback: 978-1-84694-676-9 ebook: 978-1-78099-010-1

Capitalist Realism
Is there no alternative?
Mark Fisher
An analysis of the ways in which capitalism has presented itself
as the only realistic political-economic system.
Paperback: 978-1-84694-317-1 ebook: 978-1-78099-734-6

Rebel Rebel
Chris O'Leary
David Bowie: every single song. Everything you want to know,
everything you didn't know.
Paperback: 978-1-78099-244-0 ebook: 978-1-78099-713-1

Cartographies of the Absolute
Alberto Toscano, Jeff Kinkle
An aesthetics of the economy for the twenty-first century.
Paperback: 978-1-78099-275-4 ebook: 978-1-78279-973-3

Malign Velocities
Accelerationism and Capitalism
Benjamin Noys
Long listed for the Bread and Roses Prize 2015, *Malign Velocities* argues against the need for speed, tracking acceleration as the symptom of the ongoing crises of capitalism.
Paperback: 978-1-78279-300-7 ebook: 978-1-78279-299-4

Meat Market
Female Flesh under Capitalism
Laurie Penny
A feminist dissection of women's bodies as the fleshy fulcrum of capitalist cannibalism, whereby women are both consumers and consumed.
Paperback: 978-1-84694-521-2 ebook: 978-1-84694-782-7

Poor but Sexy
Culture Clashes in Europe East and West
Agata Pyzik
How the East stayed East and the West stayed West.
Paperback: 978-1-78099-394-2 ebook: 978-1-78099-395-9

Romeo and Juliet in Palestine
Teaching Under Occupation
Tom Sperlinger
Life in the West Bank, the nature of pedagogy and the role of a university under occupation.
Paperback: 978-1-78279-637-4 ebook: 978-1-78279-636-7